How to Store Your Home-Grown Produce

About the Authors

John Harrison, who has been described as "Britain's greatest allotment authority" (*Independent on Sunday*), lives in the north-west of England with his wife Val.

They aim to be as self-sufficient as they can. John grows fruit and vegetables on two allotments, which provide much of the food they eat.

Val tends to run the kitchen, making her own jams and preserves from the home-grown produce.

This is their second collaboration, following on from *Easy Jams, Chutneys and Preserves*.

John has written three books on growing your own, including the bestselling *Vegetable Growing Month by Month* and a book on self-sufficiency *Low Cost Living*.

Together they run the much-visited website **www.allotment.org.uk**

How to Store Your Home-Grown Produce

John and Val Harrison

ROBINSON

First published in Great Britain in 2010 by Right Way,
an imprint of Constable & Robinson Ltd

This edition published in Great Britain in 2017 by Robinson

1   3   5   7   9   10   8   6   4   2

A CIP catalogue record for this book
is available from the British Library.

ISBN: 978-1-4721-4153-8

Typeset by Basement Press, Glaisdale

Printed and bound in Barcelona by Liberdúplex SL

Robinson
An imprint of
Little, Brown Book Group
Carmelite House
50 Victoria Embankment
London EC4Y 0DZ

An Hachette UK Company
www.hachette.co.uk

www.littlebrown.co.uk

Contents

Introduction

●

Over the last one hundred years we've seen a revolution in the way our food is produced, how it is stored and distributed and, above all, in our attitudes and relationship with our food. In many ways this revolution has brought improvements. We are able to go to a shop at any hour of the day or night and buy almost any fresh produce regardless of the season. Ready prepared meals that can be taken from fridge or freezer arrive on the table via the microwave within minutes.

Yet despite this "best of all possible worlds" more and more people are growing their own food. The reason is, we believe, that people want to be in control of exactly what goes into their food, and not rely on a manufacturer who may add preservatives, colorants and anti-oxidants.

Those fresh strawberries and tomatoes at Christmas no longer amaze us but we realize that however good they may look, they lack the basic quality of flavour. That's before we even begin to consider food air-miles and the carbon cost of growing out of season.

Whatever the actual reason, the fact is that we're growing our own, cutting out all the middle men and carbon costs, and ensuring the quality, safety and flavour of the food we eat.

Growing our own food has created a problem for us though: how do we store the fruits of our labour? When the potatoes are dug up, how should they be kept to last until the day, many months later, when the new potatoes arrive? What should we do with those green beans awaiting harvest when the family cries, "Enough for now!"

That's the purpose of this book: to show you the best way to store your produce so you can enjoy your green beans in the depths of winter and keep those potatoes until the new crops arrive.

These are skills that our grandparents and great-grandparents took for granted but have been lost for many of us as our parents felt they no longer needed them and didn't pass them on.

That's not to say this is a nostalgic, "how the Victorians or pioneers did it" book. Far from that, it's a practical manual firmly based in the twenty-first, not the nineteenth, century. The means to store our food practically and safely are more available and affordable now than ever before.

Perhaps most importantly is the availability of a freezer at an affordable price. We take refrigeration for granted nowadays. Do you know anyone living in a house without a fridge? Yet in living memory home fridges were not all that common and were very expensive to buy.

Of course, there are green issues with freezing. The process uses water and electricity which is the argument against. On the other side of the coin, home-grown produce doesn't attract food miles and that has to more than balance out the equation.

Some of the old methods such as drying foods are now much easier to undertake thanks to modern developments. An electrically powered food dryer can be picked up very cheaply or you can even build a drying cabinet yourself with a little ingenuity and skill.

In a nutshell, we can keep the virtues of growing and storing our own foods with far less effort and a far higher standard of hygiene than that available to our grandparents and their ancestors. This book shows you how to do it.

Measurements and Transatlantic Translation

In writing this, we're very aware that it will be published on both sides of the Atlantic. Now George Bernard Shaw famously said that, "England and America are two countries separated by a common language." How true!

We've tried to use both names for the same thing where appropriate, such as rutabaga in the USA but swede in Britain, or eggplant and aubergine. There's also confusion over the terms "bottling" and "canning". In the UK the term canning would be exclusively applied to sealing the product in metal cans whereas in the USA it is used to describe the process of sealing the food in bottles as well. Basically, if you are American, where you see "bottling" referred to in the book, please think "canning". Another term used in the UK is a Kilner jar. In the US this would be known as a Mason jar or possibly Ball jar. Whatever the name, we're talking of the same thing – glass canning or bottling jars.

Unfortunately, with measurements it's a little more tricky. We tend to use imperial measurements at home – pints and gallons, ounces and pounds – but our younger readers are happier with litres and grams or kilograms.

To further confuse the issue, a US pint is equivalent to 1.2 pints in the UK, a significant difference. Cups are always a US measurement, by the way, 8 fluid ounces.

Sometimes the difference is negligible, a US fluid ounce is very slightly less than an imperial fluid ounce but a US pint is 16 fluid ounces whilst an imperial pint is 20 fluid ounces or 1.2 US pints.

We've provided a conversion chart to help you at the end of the book and in recipes tried to include all three systems: Imp (Imperial), US and metric. When using the recipes or formulae, stick to the one system. Don't mix your imperial ounces, American quarts and metric kilos!

1
Health and Safety

●

There are times in the UK where we feel oppressed by the health and safety culture. Children are stopped from playing traditional games at school in case they hurt themselves, benches removed from parks for being 3 inches below minimum height, thereby potentially endangering the less-able elderly when they stand back up, and ornaments removed from a garden of rest as a hazard.

However mad the health and safety culture generally may seem, we think it is worth briefly discussing here as there are some risks when you are processing your produce for storage. After all, there's no need to take unnecessary risks with your family's health and welfare.

The kitchen, being the heart of the home, tends to be the busiest room in the house and inevitably ends up with more clutter than anywhere else. From those keys on the counter to the children's toys on the floor, it just seems to accumulate clutter.

Now most processing of food will involve large pots and pans of boiling water or chutney and moving around the room. It really is a recipe for an accident. So the first rule is to clear the decks for action. Tidy everything up and you won't be tripping over that toy as you move a pan to the sink.

The next rule is to exclude the children and pets, or at least make sure they're aware that they mustn't get under your feet. Our child is now grown up and away but we still have mad cats who decide that the best game is to weave through our legs at the worst possible moment. The consequences of tripping over carrying two gallons of boiling water do not bear thinking about.

Once you've cleared the surfaces, wash them down well. Most food preserving consists of preventing microbes from getting into the food and preventing the growth of those that get through our first line of defence. There's not much you can do about the spores that invisibly float in the air but clean work surfaces are easily taken care of.

We're not looking to replicate a sterile operating theatre, but freshly cleaned conditions will reduce the amount of microbes and spores dramatically. Even if it looks perfectly clean, a quick wipe over with a clean cloth and some anti-bacterial cleaner will make a huge difference.

We say a clean cloth because one of the worst sources of bacteria in the kitchen is the dishcloth. The cloth sits there, nice and damp with old bits of food at room temperature providing the perfect growth medium for bacteria.

We soak our cloth overnight in a very dilute bleach solution and hang it over the tap to dry in the day when not in use. Not only does it look clean – and don't forget you cannot see bacteria without a microscope – but it is clean.

When making preserves, give the pots, pans and utensils a wash before you start. They have sat in the closet since they were last used, accumulating dust and microbes. There's always a spot you missed when washing last time before you put the pan away and that spot of jam is happily sitting there growing fungus. We know it takes an extra ten minutes and you want to get on, but trust us it's worth it. When you realize that you've just made a batch of strawberry and spider jam, you will wish you had taken the time.

After making preserves, don't leave the pots and utensils. Washing them immediately before residues have set is far easier than it will be in a few hours' time. Having burned jam onto the bottom of a pan (we all make mistakes!) it can be very difficult to remove. Add some biological washing powder to the pan, fill with water and bring to the boil. Leave overnight and you will find the burned residue comes off reasonably easily using some wire wool or scouring pads.

With canning or bottling, making jams and preserves you will have a number of very hot jars sitting around cooling. It's all too easy to forget they're hot. Picking up a hot jar once is a mistake you won't make again. You have been warned!

We have made our own preserves and jams for many years and there are times when things go wrong. Perhaps we hurried the sterilizing or perhaps the lid wasn't on as well as we thought. Whatever the reason, it happens to everyone no matter how experienced.

If you open a preserve or some canned fruit and it doesn't smell right or you see some mould growing on the surface, then don't trust it. By preserving your own foods you are taking responsibility for their quality. When you grow and preserve food you become very aware of its value and are reluctant to throw food away, but food poisoning is no joke and it's not worth risking your family's health.

Botulism

We regularly receive letters from people worried about botulism in home preserves. Most bacterial spoilage results in a repulsive smell. The human nose is programmed to detect and reject the smells of decay but the botulism bacteria, *clostridium botulinum*, produces a neurotoxin that is so powerful it can harm you in minute amounts that you would not be aware of before eating. The bacteria is anaerobic – it does not require oxygen to grow. This makes it a particular risk with low-acid bottled or canned produce, such as beans or corn where oxygen is excluded.

It is potentially lethal and always serious but the good news is that it is exceedingly rare. According to the British National Health Service, there have been 33 cases of food borne botulism in 25 years in England and Wales and 26 of those were caused by one outbreak in commercially produced hazelnut yoghurt. Compare that to the 3,000 deaths a year in road traffic accidents in the UK and you will have an idea of the actual personal risk involved.

Following the general hygiene rules in preserving will prevent bacterial action and, therefore, reduce the risk of botulism.

Commercially canned foods undertake a "botulinum cook" whereby the temperature of the contents is raised to 121°C for three minutes. So when bottling foods susceptible to botulism (due to low acid content) raising the temperature to a high level for a short period using a purpose made canning or pressure cooker provides effective protection.

It is important to use common sense though. If you notice a pressure build up in canned or bottled produce, even if the produce seems fine − don't risk it.

One storage method where you do run a non-preventable risk of botulism is cold storing in oil. We've discussed this in more detail in the chapter on Storing in Oil.

2

What Causes Food to Ripen and Rot and How to Stop it

●

We all know that food goes off if it is kept too long but you may not have given any thought to how and why it does so. An understanding of what causes our food to deteriorate in storage will help you prevent it happening. It will also help you understand the reasons when things go wrong, as they sometimes do, when you store your produce. Incidentally, it will also help you to ripen some fruits that may have to be harvested early because of the weather, like tomatoes.

The purpose of a fruit, at least as far as the plant is concerned, is to help the seeds contained within to grow and produce new plants. You may have noticed how many ripe berries and fruit are red in colour. This signals to birds and animals that the fruit is now edible and full of nutrients for them. This is why the red berries on holly bushes are eaten by the birds before the yellow berries. (Some colours, however, like green zebra-striped tomatoes and white currants, are just sports that man is responsible for producing rather than nature itself.)

So the bird or animal comes along, and eats the fruit and the seeds contained within it. The fruit provides energy for the animal but the seed passes through the gut unharmed and is deposited inside some fertilizing manure. That's why tomatoes were often found growing wild around sewerage plants – someone had enjoyed the tomato and passed the seed along.

Unripe fruits will contain chlorophyll, starches and acids as well as having a hard texture. The ripening process breaks down the chlorophyll, which changes the colour from "unripe" green. It also changes the starches to sugars, reduces the acid content and finally softens the fruit. Plants aren't perfect though, once the fruit is perfectly ripe it doesn't stop the process. The fruit continues to soften, becoming mushy and more vulnerable to moulds and bacteria so rot sets in.

Tubers – the root crops like potatoes, carrots, parsnips, etc. – work on a different principle. They are, like bulbs, a method the plant uses to store energy so that it can carry on next year. This is useful for us in that they naturally remain dormant for the winter. If we can duplicate the winter conditions they expect, then they will remain in good condition. Once they decide that spring has sprung, they burst out of their hibernation and start to use their stored goodness to produce new plants and seed heads. They don't rot as such, but they do become inedible. Of course, if they are damaged in store, those microbes will gain access and start to consume the cells. Damage can be mechanical, cuts in the skin when harvesting, or caused by pests such as slugs feeding on the crop.

Ethylene Gas

Just as we use hormones to control the cells in our bodies, plants use hormones, and ripening is controlled by ethylene gas – the same gas that welders use but in much smaller quantities, of course.

There's often a benefit to the plant if a lot of its fruits ripen at once. A whole vine of tomatoes or bunch of bananas will be noticeable to animals from a longer distance than a single tomato or banana. So when one tomato starts to produce a little ethylene, this not only triggers it to ripen but also encourages the other fruit nearby to start producing the gas and ripen as well in a chain reaction.

This is useful to supermarkets and greengrocers as they can import fruit in an unripe state and then ripen it when they want to put it on the shelf. We can use this hormone control at home with a lot of fruits to get them to ripen when we want. Placing a ripe banana (which produces quite a lot of ethylene gas) in a bowl of green tomatoes will cause them to start ripening. If you have a bunch of green bananas, placing them in a plastic bag will increase the concentration of the gas and they'll quickly ripen.

To prevent fruit from ripening, the distributors will control the temperature and atmosphere so the ethylene gas density is kept very low. Controlling temperature at home is fairly easy – we put things in the fridge – but until recently reducing ethylene was not possible. In fact, keeping things in a fridge meant the gas was concentrated, which worked against us. However, there is now a product on the market in Britain called the Ethylene Gas Guardian (EGG) that absorbs the gas into a mineral, zeolite.

There are a number of fruits that give off ethylene and the list below shows the most common:

Very High Ethylene Producers	High Ethylene Producers	Medium Ethylene Producers
Apples	Apricots	Bananas
Passion Fruit	Avocado Pears	Mangoes
	Nectarines	Melons
	Peaches	Plums
	Pears	Tomatoes

Surprisingly, ethylene causes significant loss of condition in a much wider range of fruit and vegetables including:

Apples	Cucumbers	Passion Fruit
Apricots	Kiwifruit	Peaches
Avocados	Lettuce and Leaf Salads	Pears
Bananas	Mangoes	Plums
Broccoli	Melons	Quinces
Brussels Sprouts	Nectarines	Tomatoes

Dehydration

Fresh fruit and vegetables mainly consist of water. The exact percentage varies but typically 80 to 95 per cent. As they dry out, they lose condition and quite a small amount of loss is enough to make them unappealing at least.

Dehydration is the reason that lettuce goes limp. The stiffness of the leaves (and the crunch) depends on the pressure of water in the plant and like a balloon deflating so the leaves crumple in. This happens faster in leafy vegetables as they have more surface area to lose water from but all vegetables will dry out to some degree while in store.

Maintaining a humid atmosphere helps reduce dehydration but conversely encourages the growth of moulds and fungi.

Although controlled dehydration is a method of preserving food this partial dehydration can cause damage to the crop. The main structure collapses as do individual cells. This allows mould spores and bacteria to get in and there is enough water left to allow them to grow and spoil the food.

Moulds, Fungi and Bacteria

The biggest cause of storage loss is due to microbial action. As food ripens, the conditions become more and more suitable for them to

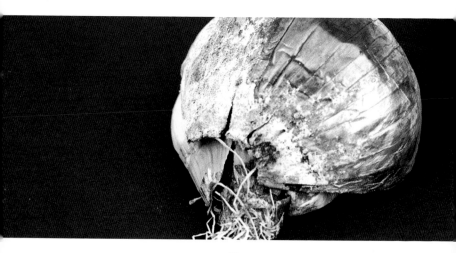

grow. The sugars provide energy for them, the acidity falls which helps them and cell walls break down as the fruit softens, making it easier for them to get in.

Most preserving methods concentrate on preventing spores and microbes getting to the food and those that may already be there from developing and growing. Our air is full of these microscopic trouble makers but they don't cause any trouble to us until they grow and multiply manyfold on our food source. We cover how each preserving method prevents bacterial and mould growth in the relevant chapters.

Unlike meat, usually with fruit and vegetables by the time bacteria have become a problem the other effects of over-ripening and spoilage have made the food inedible anyway.

Oxygen

Most of the microbes that damage our foods depend, as we do, on oxygen to grow. Excluding oxygen will, therefore, stop those microbes from growing. Many preserving methods depend, to some extent, on excluding oxygen because of this.

There is a trend now for stores to sell salad leaves in sealed bags. If you put your salad leaves into a sealed plastic bag for a week, you'll find that a sludgy and very smelly mess is the result. The commercial producers have replaced the air in the bag with an inert gas, usually nitrogen. Personally we prefer fresh.

Enzymatic Action

Simply put, if only because we're not biologists, enzymes are molecules that enable other chemical actions involved in ripening our fruits. Generally they make no difference to us as the preserving processes stop those chemical reactions. Although there is one exception that we should be aware of: freezing. Freezing stops bacterial action completely and so food is safe to eat however long it is frozen for. Nevertheless, freezing only slows enzymes down so the flavour and texture of frozen food can deteriorate over time. Boiling destroys the enzymes so the process stops which is why you should blanch the bulk of frozen foods.

3
Where to Store

•

W hen you start seriously growing your own, you hit the problem of where to keep your produce. The modern house is designed for a modern lifestyle of 24 hour shopping and kitchens with storage are kept nice and warm by the house heating system. Just the wrong conditions for the long-term storage of our crops.

Pre-war houses in the UK usually came with a larder – a purpose-built room off the kitchen with just a small window for ventilation and a marble cold shelf across the back. Now it's likely that larder has been knocked through to increase the size of the kitchen and all we have left is a fridge in the nice warm kitchen. This causes us a bit of a problem when we have a year's supply of vegetables to keep.

Cellars

In North America many rural properties benefited from a purpose-built root cellar. Because these were, at least partially, underground they provided the ideal storage for the home-grown produce. In hot summer months the root cellar would remain relatively cool and in the harsh winter relatively warm.

Don't forget, for many of those early American homesteaders, keeping their produce in good condition was a matter of survival. Badly designed root cellars would not just be an annoyance, the food inside was keeping them alive.

Nowadays, on both sides of the Atlantic, cellars are rare and purpose-designed root cellars rarer still. However, if you do have a cellar, then it may well be utilized for storage.

Unheated cellars are best, of course. The ideal temperature for our needs is between 1°C and 10°C (34–40°F). Below this our produce freezes and above this the storage life goes down.

Many cellars have become part of the house and are heated or at least contain the boiler (furnace in the USA) which will radiate heat. In this case, as we cover below, the answer is to build a separate room or large cupboard in the cellar that can be kept cool.

Although some humidity is good for storing, a damp cellar is not what we want. You'll notice that damp cellars tend to have mould growing on the walls and mould is an enemy of stored food. So if your cellar is really damp, this needs addressing before you start storing in there.

Our cellar needs some ventilation. Vegetables continue to breathe when in store and will give off moisture in the process. If our cellar is bone dry but airtight, this moisture will make it a damp mould-breeding ground in short order. A small window, screened to keep vermin out or even just some ventilation bricks, is enough to allow the air to change and take excess moisture away.

The final need for our food storage is to be vermin free. The last thing you want to find is a family of mice or rats living off your hard-won crop.

Attics or Lofts

In the absence of a cellar, we need to find somewhere else to store our produce. In the modern home our options are somewhat limited and we need to adapt.

An attic or loft can sometimes be converted to provide a food store or have an area of it adapted for the purpose. The problem with an attic is that it can be very awkward to access. Taking sacks of potatoes and boxes of carrots up a flight of stairs and then up a ladder gets tiresome pretty quickly.

As we've improved home insulation levels, our attics have become much colder places as well. Remember we don't want the temperature below freezing in our food store, so we can end up actually removing insulation between the attic and the house. In very cold areas, you may well need to provide additional insulation surrounding the area used as a food store to avoid it becoming a freezer.

Getting the ventilation right in an attic can be troublesome as well. Having run through the general drawbacks, your own situation may be different, but we ruled out using our attic for those reasons.

Spare Rooms

It may be that you have a spare bedroom or box room that can be used as your store. Don't forget that root crops will inevitably involve soil and you may not want to trek it through the house and up and down the stairs. A bedroom is likely to be warmer than ideal, even with heating turned off in the room. It's surprising how warm a room actually is even though it feels freezing when you walk in from the warm house.

Converting an Existing Building or Room

It's hardly practical and certainly doesn't make economic sense to construct a full-scale new root cellar in a property, even assuming you can get the required permits and permissions.

The most practical answer we have found is to convert a garden shed or garage into a store. Don't forget we live in England and our winter weather is rarely very harsh. This may not be a suitable solution for those living in very cold or hot areas. We'll explain how we fitted out our shed, which is just as applicable to a garage or creating a root cellar in an existing cellar as mentioned above.

Our cool storing "root cellar" is just 6 feet by 5 feet and sits in our large garden shed. We constructed it in the corner, so we only needed to build two walls, one to the side and one to the front with a door.

The walls need not be anything fancy. Some plywood panel shuttering supported on a frame of 2 x 2s will be adequate as they are not load bearing. We actually constructed ours from scrap timber we had lying around.

The next job was to insulate. Insulation will help keep the cold out in winter and the warmth out in summer. How thick the insulation

needs to be will depend on how extreme your weather conditions are. We found 25 mm (1 inch) polystyrene sheets (AKA as Styrofoam or foamboard) the easiest and most economical to work with. To hold the sheets in place we just used wallpaper paste but you may need to use purpose-made adhesive, and wedged sheets in between studs. Rough and ready, but it did the job.

The type and amount of insulation you install will depend on where you are. We rarely have to cope with temperatures below −5°C (23°F) in winter here, although it has fallen to −14°C (7°F) once. If we lived somewhere where that, for us, abnormal low temperature was a regular event, we would have tripled the insulation or gone for a double-skinned wall construction filled with blown fibre or fibre glass.

If you want to keep costs to a minimum, you can insulate reasonably effectively using scrunched up newspaper inside a double-skin wall or multiple layers of corrugated cardboard. Many supermarkets will happily give you old boxes for the asking.

Having got our insulation in place, we installed a closable mesh grill in the outside wall towards the roof level and a grill in the door towards the bottom. These allow air to flow through the store, preventing a too humid atmosphere but the vents can be closed off in extremely cold conditions.

The final task was to fix up some shelving. Rather than solid shelves, we constructed slatted shelves from 2 x 1 inch timber. The slats allow air to flow through and this prevents damp building up under sacks, etc. The shelves were just fixed to the uprights of the stud wall.

The ideal storage conditions vary for different produce – root crops such as carrots like a temperature between 0°C and 4°C (32–40°F) whereas potatoes should be between 5°C and 10°C (40–50°F), all of which complicates things a little.

The fact is we are not going to achieve perfection so we just do the best we can. We keep our carrots in damp sand in boxes on the lower shelves and our potatoes in sacks on the higher shelves. Heat rises so the potatoes are slightly warmer.

On the side without a shelf we attached hooks from which we can hang strings of onions, garlic and netted shallots, etc.

As we said above, the storage area should ideally be kept between 1°C and 10°C (34–40°F). Since our storeroom is mainly used through the winter, keeping us supplied until the new crops start to arrive in late spring and early summer, too hot is rarely a problem. Too cold, however, is a problem. If your onions or potatoes freeze, they are ruined. The cells will have burst due to the ice crystals forming and when they defrost they will be mushy and start to rot in short order.

Our answer to this was to heat the storeroom for those days when the outdoor temperature dropped very low. It doesn't take much energy to keep such a small volume above freezing. We have a small paraffin heater designed to keep a coldframe warm but the problem with this, and with propane gas heaters, is they require fresh air to avoid producing carbon monoxide and they give off moisture. The last thing we want is to make our storeroom damp and encourage moulds to grow.

Electricity was the only practical answer. You can buy low-powered, thermostatically controlled electric heaters designed for greenhouses. Generally these consume around 100 watts. Don't forget they only switch on when needed, so the actual power consumption is not so bad.

We built our own heater utilizing a thermostat purchased for pennies at a garage sale, a metal cookie tin box and a light bulb holder. The thermostat switches on when the temperature falls and allows the 60 watt light to come on inside the tin box. We poked holes through the top of the tin and around the base to allow air to be drawn in, heated and then to flow out through the lid to heat the room.

Normally this is perfectly sufficient for cold nights but when we had our abnormally cold spell, it couldn't maintain the temperature and we had to swap it for a thermostatically controlled room heater for a few days.

Incidentally, before installing electrical points, etc., do check that your local laws allow you to do so. Some jurisdictions insist that a qualified person undertakes electrical works or a licensed person performs the hook-ups.

4
Natural Storage

●

Vegetable Clamps and Pits

The clamp is an outdoor storage method for root crops such as potatoes, carrots, swedes, beetroot and celeriac. It goes back hundreds of years and was commonly in use until the 1950s. Clamps were more used by farmers than home growers, but the farmers now use climate controlled storage and the home grower has other, more convenient and efficient, methods available.

Clamps are not really useful for today's small families as they need quite a large quantity of whatever crop to build. However, they do have a use if you are storing animal fodder crops, like horse carrots.

The drawbacks with the traditional clamp are that the stored produce is subject to damage by pests and extreme weather. They are vulnerable to insects, especially to slugs and vermin like rats. In very cold weather the contents may well freeze and in very wet weather become damp and rot off.

In building a clamp, the first thing to ensure is that the crop will be kept out of standing water. Choose a dry spot in the garden or plot and then dig a trench around the storage area. This will help drain any water and provides soil you will need later to cover the clamp.

Next, place a thick layer of straw, bracken or even shredded paper on the ground and then place a layer of your crop down. With carrots, you could try a circular pattern, thick end to the outside, then place another layer of your packing material or sharp sand to level up. You need washed river sand as any salt will suck moisture out of the produce. Carry on adding layers to form a cone shape.

On the outside of the clamp, place 6 to 8 inches of straw and make a little straw spike at the top. This is to allow excess moisture to escape.

The soil you removed from your drainage trench can then be used to cover the clamp, although you will need more from elsewhere in the garden.

A more modern version of the clamp is to use a sheet of plastic or vinyl under the base straw as a water barrier and to cover the clamp with a thick sheet of plastic or vinyl to stop rain soaking it in very wet weather. However, covering with vinyl does prevent any moisture escaping except through your straw vent which may not be enough to stop your store rotting.

A variation on the clamp is to dig a storage pit. Usually this would be some 2 feet (60 cm) deep and around 2 feet x 4 feet (60 cm x 1.2 m) in area. The sides need to be supported – anything from bricks or concrete blocks to plywood panels can be used – and the floor covered.

You then need to construct some sort of waterproof lid, perhaps wood with plastic or roofing felt or shingles to go over. The vegetables are stored in damp sand or peat moss inside the pit. The problems with this method are water and temperature. It's far more difficult to keep out water than you might think and your box pit is like a sink, holding the water when it seeps in. You can try using old sheets of polystyrene foam board to insulate because if the temperature falls well below freezing your produce will be spoilt.

We cannot wholeheartedly recommend either of these methods for the ordinary home grower but include them here as we are often asked about them.

Storing Roots in Sand, Peat, Etc.

This traditional method of storing, which we do recommend, is effective for many of the root crops and will keep them in good condition for months. The reason is that we are working with nature.

If you think about the carrot or parsnip in the wild, it forms a good strong root in its first year which then sits in the ground for the winter. The next spring it bursts back into life and uses the stored energy in the root to fuel putting up a seed head and starting the next generation.

What we do for these root crops is to provide them with the ideal winter conditions so they lie dormant until we want to eat them. Remember, the root isn't dead; it's actually hibernating and so still needs some moisture to keep it ticking over.

Instead of soil, which would contain pests that would damage our produce, we use a variety of materials to hold some moisture around our crop. Clean sand (it must not have any salt in it because salt will suck moisture out of the root) or peat are most commonly used. You can use sawdust or even sterile compost.

We've found peat moss to be the best but there are environmental concerns about depleting peat stocks. However, you can buy peat moss that is filtered from river water thereby not contributing to the depletion and, of course, we are re-using the peat moss year after year.

Take a box large enough for your crop and put a layer of your preferred filler on the base. This material just needs to be damp, not wet. If you can squeeze water out of it in your hand, it is too wet. Allow it to dry out a little before using in that case.

Remove the foliage just above the crown and then place a row of carrots, for example, top to tail to get the most in there but not actually touching each other. Pour your sand or peat or whatever over, covering by half an inch and then repeat, making sure the last layer is covered to exclude light.

As you remove from the box to eat, check that the remaining produce is still well covered.

The trigger that causes the root to come back to life is temperature. Once the temperature rises, your roots will start to wake up and sprout leaves and a seed head which will use the goodness in the root, making it of no value to you to eat. The ideal storage temperature is just above freezing, between 0°C and 4°C (32–40°F).

If you have still got a fair amount in storage when the warmer weather arrives and you can't maintain a low temperature, it's best to remove the crop from the box and freeze or otherwise store it.

Crops suitable for storing this way include:

- Carrots
- Parsnips
- Beetroots (beets)
- Swedes (rutabaga)
- Turnips

Usually you would use maincrop/later varieties rather than the types bred to be eaten young. Young carrots, beets and turnips are better stored in other ways.

5
Salting

•

Salting food to preserve it goes back at least as far as the Middle Ages and probably much further since the Romans were known to mine large quantities of salt in Cheshire, England as well as producing it by evaporating sea water.

Although salting is mainly associated with meat and fish, it can be used to preserve vegetables. The salt draws moisture out of food by a process known as osmosis. The easy way to demonstrate osmosis is to put a little pile of salt or a sugar lump by a drop of water. The water will be quickly sucked into the salt.

The salt will also actually suck moisture out of the cells of bacteria and microbes, effectively killing them. Killing and preventing the growth of microbes stops them from spoiling food.

Salting vegetables is rare nowadays, which is due to the fuss involved in preparing the salted vegetables for use and concerns about too much salt in the diet. High salt intake has been shown to be related to high blood pressure, strokes and cardiovascular disease. Don't think that salt is bad for you. We need salt to live. However, the problem arises from too much salt in our diet according to scientists. Strangely this conclusion is contested by the Salt Manufacturers Association in the UK!

It's important to realize that most of that salt we consume in our modern diet comes from processed foods. Seventy-five per cent of our salt intake comes to us that way according to the Food Standards Agency. A single tin of baked beans may contain over half (3.4 mg) of our recommended daily allowance of 6 mg.

With many "ready meals" the amount of salt and sugar is huge, far greater than you would add when cooking yourself. The reason is that it is a cheap and easy way for the manufacturer to create flavour, balancing the high sugar with high levels of salt.

While you can store a range of vegetables by salting, our experience is that it does not give the best result with one exception. Runner or French beans really do store well in salt, keeping their colour and flavour while avoiding the softening that freezing produces.

Salted Beans

The ideal container to use is a Kilner-style wide-mouthed jar made of glass. Never use metal containers as the salt concentration seems to absorb a metallic taste. Although the salt will preserve the beans, you will need to exclude light to keep the colour. So either store in a completely dark cupboard or wrap the jars with brown paper when filled.

We've read that you should use Kosher or preserving salt for the beans but we found the cheapest salt on the store shelf did the job perfectly well. You definitely don't need to pay for special sea salts or such like; just the cheapest food grade salt is fine.

Rinse your beans and slice runners diagonally and into one inch lengths, just "top and tail" and then cut French beans to a length that will lie flat in the jar. Start with a thin layer of salt, then add a layer of beans and then cover with salt. Keep repeating until your jar is full, finishing with a layer of salt, put the lid on and then wrap and place into store.

As you fill the jar, do press down well to compress the contents. If you don't fill your jar in one go, you can add more as the next flush of beans becomes available to harvest. Leave half an inch of headroom in the jar before putting the lid on as the contents can expand a little as the salt absorbs moisture.

The ideal ratio is about 450 g of salt to 1.35 kg of beans (1 lb to 3 lb) but you need not be too exact. You'll notice that the salt becomes

damp, sometimes sludge like, as it sucks the moisture from the beans. Don't worry; this is normal.

Be careful when storing and removing your beans from the jar as the very salty liquid can attack the glaze on some tiles.

When you use the beans, remove from the jar and soak for no more than three quarters of an hour in clean cold water. Soaking for too long will toughen the beans. Rinse off under running cold water and then cook as normal, remembering you will not need to add any salt when cooking.

6
Lacto-Fermentation

●

Although the name "lacto-fermentation" sounds like something that should be undertaken by men in white coats in a laboratory, it's actually just the technical name for the process by which sauerkraut is made, converting some sugars to lactic acid through fermentation as a preservative.

Sauerkraut

Although in the UK we tend to think of sauerkraut as a German dish, it's actually a traditional preserving method for cabbage popular across Eastern Europe and the USA. Its history is supposed to date back two thousand years to ancient China with the method reaching Europe via Genghis Khan and his hordes' invasions in the thirteenth century.

Variations on European sauerkraut in the east include the Japanese Tsukemono pickle and Korean kim chi. In Korea kim chi is served with nearly every meal including breakfast which can give visitors a bit of a shock. It's very much an acquired taste!

Sauerkraut is not complicated to produce, only requiring cabbage and salt to draw out the juices from the cabbage which then ferment due to their sugar content. The fermentation produces lactic acid and the acidic conditions prevent microbial growth as well as being responsible for the distinctive flavour.

Sauerkraut is actually quite a healthy food, the main ingredient being cabbage which is rich in vitamins, particularly vitamin C. The Dutch navy used to take sauerkraut on their ships to prevent scurvy in much the same way as we used to take limes.

The fermentation process produces isothiocyanates which have been shown to prevent cancer in laboratory animals, so may well be helpful for us. Homemade sauerkraut stored in a fridge also contains pro-biotic bacteria which assist in digestion although the heating involved in bottling kills these.

You need quite a large cylindrical crockery jar or pot. You can ferment small amounts of cabbage but the process is more reliable with a reasonable amount. As with all food preparation, pay attention to cleanliness. It's important that containers and utensils are scrupulously clean if not sterile.

Take two ball-head white cabbages; late or kraut varieties may be best as they contain more sugars for the process. Discard the outer leaves and cut out the solid stalk and any damaged bits. Weigh at this point. The recipe is based on 2.25 kg (5 lb) but you can adjust the salt quantity to match the cabbage quantity, keeping the same ratio. For bottled (canned) storage, that's 100 g per 2.25 kg (45 g per kg) or 4 oz per 5 lb, just under an ounce per pound. For refrigerated sauerkraut you can reduce the salt to 35 g per kilo, just over half an ounce per pound.

The ideal salt to use for sauerkraut is koshering salt, also known as kosher salt in the USA. It takes its name not from being a kosher food (approved for orthodox Jews) but because it is commonly used for salting meat to remove the blood which is not allowed in kosher foods.

It's pretty difficult to find kosher salt in the UK, if not impossible, so just use a coarse salt without added iodine; sea salt is usually the best. Ordinary table salt will do but purists say it changes the flavour, not that we noticed any great difference.

Prepare your cabbage by shredding. You can use a knife or a mandolin but the easiest method is in batches in a food processor.

Take a large non-metal mixing bowl and layer some cabbage, then sprinkle with salt and repeat until everything is in the bowl. Then mix thoroughly with a wooden spoon or your hands. After the cabbage is prepared, avoid touching it with any metal and particularly aluminium utensils which may react with the acid generated.

After half an hour or so, the cabbage will have wilted somewhat, which means the volume will have decreased. At this point, scrape all the contents and pour all the liquid that will have started into your crockery jar.

Press down firmly as you pack your jar with the back of the spoon. You should see the liquid rise to the top, covering the cabbage. If there isn't enough liquor to cover the cabbage, add a little brine until covered. You make the brine by adding 20 g of salt to 500 ml of hot water (a generous half ounce per imperial pint or three quarters of an ounce per US pint). Mix well and allow to cool before using.

Now we want to keep the cabbage compressed and sealed to prevent moulds or yeasts getting in. After trying various methods involving plates and weights, we came across the easy and effective method of filling a plastic bag with water and placing this on the top. The bag will shape itself to the edges of the jar and the weight of water compresses the sauerkraut.

It's a good idea to double bag the water; if the water leaks into the jar the sauerkraut will be ruined.

Cover the bag and top of the jar with cling-film wrap, leaving some slack for gasses produced by the fermentation to go into, and cover with a heavy tea-towel. Place in a cool place; the ideal temperature is around 16°C (61°F). Too cold and the fermentation will be very slow, while higher temperatures impair the flavour. Above 25°C (77°F) the bacteria will be killed stopping fermentation altogether.

Check how things are progressing every week. If a scum has developed on the surface of the brine, skim this off with a spoon but don't expose the cabbage. After five weeks your sauerkraut should be ready. Taste a little to see. Once ready, keep the jar covered in a very cold place or the fridge, removing the sauerkraut as required for eating with a slotted spoon. It should keep well for two months, possibly three.

For longer term storage, bottling (canning) is the answer. Allow slightly longer fermentation if you intend to bottle as the bottling (canning) mellows the flavour so you want to make it slightly more tart than you want it to taste when finally eaten.

Wash and sterilize your jars in the oven whilst bringing your sauerkraut and the brine to a boil in a stainless steel pan. Stir frequently to avoid burning. Pack into the jars, leaving a little headspace, about 1 cm (half an inch), before sealing.

Flavoured Sauerkraut

We've given the basic recipe but you can flavour your sauerkraut in a number of ways. Adding sliced apples (about 3 apples to the standard recipe), juniper berries, bay leaves, garlic, grated carrots, shredded onions or a mixture of the above are all used.

Korean kim chi is a variant on sauerkraut made hot (often blisteringly hot) with the addition of crushed chilli peppers along with garlic, ginger, onions, cucumber and even citrus fruit. If you like sauerkraut and also like hot foods such as curries, give it a try. As with all experiments, sometimes the result is fantastic and sometimes a failure. Keep a note of the recipe you use so if you hit what you think is a winner, you can replicate it.

7

Bottling (Canning)

●

One thing that used to confuse us was receiving emails from the USA referring to canning. Finally we realized that our American correspondents were referring to what we in Britain would call bottling.

You can, of course, store foods in tin cans at home just as the commercial producers of tinned food do but you need a source of cans and lids plus a machine to join the two together. My grandmother related how the Americans had sent over domestic scale canning machines in World War Two but eventually the cans ran out and people just went back to bottling. We're not aware of anybody selling domestic canning machines in the UK although they may still be available in the USA.

The preservative method of bottling is straightforward. The produce is heated to kill off any microbes in either a syrup, for fruits, or a brine for vegetables and then sealed to keep out new microbes and exclude oxygen.

The concept goes right back to the Greeks and Romans who discovered that excluding air was a key to keeping foods edible for long periods. However, their success rates were probably not so high as excluding the air is not as easy as it seems.

A glazed jar was used with a glazed lid but sealing the two was the problem. Various items were tried, ranging from wax to stretched pig's bladders but, without any knowledge of bacteria or sterilization, their preserved foods would often go off and eating them was a game of Russian roulette.

As so often happens, war was the driving force for an invention. An army marches on its stomach and getting food to the troops was the reason that, in 1800, Napoleon Bonaparte offered a 12,000 franc reward to anyone who could devise a method for the preservation of food that would help provide his troops with daily rations and thereby keep his army adequately supplied.

After years of experimentation, Nicolas Appert submitted his invention of bottling and won the prize in 1809. Ironically it was a year later that an Englishman, Peter Durand, adapted the process. He placed wholesome food in clean metal containers, which were then sealed and boiled long enough to kill the spoilage-causing micro organisms. These were similar in shape to tea canisters and the name "can" came into common parlance.

After 1900, home bottling of all types of food became popular as a means of safely storing home garden products, providing better diets, and reducing the cost of living.

In the USA home canning, using special equipment in actual tin cans, became quite widespread. However, the requirement for the special sealing equipment and the high cost of single use cans, when compared with re-usable bottles, caused a decline in its practice. Nevertheless, the description "canning" stuck to home bottling which remained popular there, as it is in the UK. To avoid too much repetition, we would ask our American readers just to think "canning" whenever we refer to "bottling".

Bottled fruits are very useful in the store cupboard. You can make them into a whole range of desserts from apple crumble to rhubarb pie. Don't forget that they also make an unusual and practical gift – all the benefits of home grown with the convenience of store bought.

Safety of Bottled Food

While the process is very effective, things can go wrong. As with all food preservation, hygiene and attention to detail are critical for successful and safe storage.

One obvious risk is the seal breaking and allowing microbes access to the food. These will develop and produce gas, often leading to an increase in pressure. With commercial canned goods where the tin has been damaged, a sure sign the contents are spoiled is the can swelling. In the grocery trade, they're known as "blown".

If you open a home bottled jar and there's a release of pressure, the food is spoiled. Usually the obnoxious smell will make this very obvious but please don't trust the food even if it smells OK. The simple rule is to ask, "Would I be happy with this if I'd bought it from a shop?"

As we covered in Chapter 1, the risk of botulism is very small. That's not to say impossible. It is difficult to draw a balance in writing this book when warning you of possible risks. We ourselves have never actually had a problem so we don't want to overstate the risks, but they do exist if you ignore the rules.

Bottles or Jars

Before you start bottling, do check your jars. You need solid, thick glass jars which are sold under the Kilner or Le Parfait brands in the UK or known as Mason jars in the US. If you already have jars, check the condition – especially around the lip. Any chips or cracks make them unusable. Rubber seals that go between lid and jar must be in good condition as well. These sealing rings do deteriorate and can stretch with time which prevents a good, safe seal but are relatively inexpensive to replace if you shop around. Ensure you get the correct size though, you won't get away with the wrong ones.

Metal lids and screw rings/bands should be clean and corrosion free. A smear of Vaseline on the outside is good for preventing corrosion.

The most useful sizes of jars are half quart or quart size (500 ml or 1 litre). There are two main types on the market:

- **Spring-Clip Top bottles** – Normally have a glass top and a rubber ring between the lid and the rim of the bottle. This helps to form a complete seal when the bottle has been processed.
- **Screw Band bottles** – Usually have a glass or metal lid fitted with a rubber ring kept in place by a band which screws on.

During processing (except with the oven method) this band should be loosely screwed on and then tightened while the bottle is cooling.

Bottling Utensils

- **Thermometer** – Special high temperature thermometers are available for bottling and jam making and, although not essential, make life a lot easier.
- **Long-Handled Wooden Spoon** – For packing fruit into larger bottles.
- **Bottling Tongs** – Not essential but help when handling hot bottles, especially when removing them from pressure cookers or water baths.

- **Oven Mitts** – You are going to be handling hot pans and jars.
- **Large Baking Tray** – For the oven method of bottling to stand the bottles on.
- **Wire Cooling Tray or Heatproof Mats** – To put hot bottles on when cooling.
- **Large Flat-Bottomed Pan or Purpose-Made Bath Canner** – For water bath method.
- **Pressure Cooker or Canner** – For pressure method.
- **Trivet or Wire Tray for Base of Pans** – This stops the direct heat from cracking the jars during processing.
- **Timer** – Or a watch/clock with a second hand for timing.

Preparation of Fruit and Vegetables

Fruit used for bottling must be fresh, firm, and free from discoloration and disease. Wash hard fruits in cold water and leave to drain in a colander. Soft fruits can be soaked for a few minutes in salted water to remove any grubs or insects, rinsed in fresh cold water and left to drain.

When bottling in syrup, the addition of some ascorbic acid, as described in the instructions for freezing (page 131), will help to maintain colour with fruits like apples and apricots that discolour easily.

While you can bottle quite a range of vegetables, the most popular is undoubtedly the tomato. As you may know, tomatoes are technically a fruit and their high acid levels mean you can usually treat it as a fruit. However, some modern super-sweet varieties are actually low in acid so should be bottled using the pressure method as if they were a vegetable. Your seed supplier should be able to tell you if a new variety is low acid.

Pick your vegetables young and process as soon as possible after harvest. They should be thoroughly cleaned or peeled as if preparing to cook them directly. Cut into reasonable sized pieces if appropriate. It's quite a lengthy process to bottle vegetables and we would really advise freezing as being generally more appropriate. Surprisingly, you also need to blanch vegetables just as if you were freezing them to retain the colour before pressure bottling them. We've covered the method for the most popular bottling vegetables.

- **Apples and Pears** – Peel, core and cut into quarters or slices and place into lightly salted water to prevent discoloration or add some lemon juice or ascorbic acid to the water. Rinse quickly in cold water before packing in jars. For a solid pack, prepare as above and blanch in boiling water for 2 or 3 minutes or steam over boiling water until just tender. Pack warm.
- **Apricots, Peaches, Plums and Damsons** – Remove stalks and rinse. May be bottled whole or halved with the stones removed. If halved, pack quickly cut side down in jars before they discolour.
- **Strawberries** – Hull and rinse the berries carefully.
- **Blackcurrants, Redcurrants and Gooseberries** – Top and tail. Wash and drain well before packing into jars. Gooseberries can tend to wrinkle in processing. To avoid this make a nick with a knife in the bottom of the fruit.
- **Cherries** – Remove stalks and rinse.
- **Citrus Fruits** – Remove the peel and pith, break up into segments and discard any pips.
- **Blackberries, Raspberries and Loganberries** – Remove stalks and rinse. These fruits attract maggots so pick over carefully then soak in lightly salted water for 10 minutes and any bugs will float to the surface to be removed.
- **Rhubarb** – Remove leaves and base, wipe sticks and cut into even lengths suitable for the size of the bottle. Young rhubarb is sweeter and more tender than older stalks.
- **Pineapple** – Cut off the outside peel, top and tail and then slice into rings or chunks. If bottling as rings, do check that the jars are wide enough to take them.
- **Tomatoes** – Remove stems, wash in cold water and drain. Pack with or without the skins. The skins can easily be peeled off if the tomatoes are put into boiling water for 5 to 15 seconds and then dipped in cold water.

For a solid pack, cut in halves or quarters. Pack tightly in the jars, sprinkling salt on each layer. About 1 teaspoon per pound of tomatoes is all you need. If the tomatoes are very acid, you may find it worth adding a teaspoon per pound of sugar along with the salt. Press the tomatoes well down in the jars but do not add any liquid.

- **Asparagus** – Wash and trim the tough end off the stalks. The tough portion can be used in soups. Blanch the stalks and place in the jar thick end down.
- **Broad (Fava) Beans** – Remove the beans from the pods. The processing can turn the beans brown even when blanched. This seems to be related to the variety grown.
- **French and Runner Beans** – Wash, string runners, and cut to appropriate length for the jar. Blanch and pack into jars.
- **Peas** – If you have a problem with pea maggots, pod into a bowl of salted water and they will float to the top. Blanch and pack into jars.
- **Sweetcorn** – We find it easier to blanch the whole cob and then, using a sharp knife, remove the kernels which are packed into jars.
- **Sweet Peppers** – With peppers it can be easiest to quarter and de-seed, then blanch and remove the outer skin before bottling rather than trying to remove the skin before blanching.

Bottling Syrup

Fruit may be bottled in syrup, water or a brine solution. Syrup is preferable as it helps to preserve the colour and flavour. The strength of the syrup depends on the sweetness of the fruit and how it is packed. For syrups the proportions are generally 250 g to 600 ml of water (9 oz per Imp pint, 8 oz per US pint).

The sugar for use in syrups may be ordinary white granulated or, for a different flavour, honey or golden syrup. Dissolve the sugar in half of the water over a moderate heat and, when the sugar is dissolved, boil for one minute. Then add the remainder of the water. Doing it this way saves time in waiting for the syrup to cool sufficiently for use.

Bottling Brine for Tomatoes, etc.

A brine solution is best for tomatoes and vegetables. Make it with 30 g of salt to 1 litre of water (1 oz per 1¾ Imp pints or 2 US pints). If they are to be packed solidly no water is necessary but 1 teaspoon of salt should be added to each 450 g (1 lb) of tomatoes.

Methods of Bottling

There are a number of methods of bottling. The method to use will depend on what produce you are bottling and your own preference. However, for bottling vegetables where they have low acidity and there is, therefore, a definite botulism risk, you must use the pressure method to ensure your safety.

With all methods, ensure the jars and lids are scrupulously clean before you start. If you have a dishwasher, running them through it on the hottest cycle or even a sterilize cycle is a real time saver. Otherwise, wash by hand in soapy water as hot as you can, rinse and scald with boiling water.

Packing the contents in when the jars are wet will help things slide in, using your wooden spoon to pack tightly. Soft fruits should be packed as tightly as possible in layers without squashing and adding syrup or water every four or five layers.

Hard fruits may be pressed down with the handle of a wooden spoon and the syrup or water poured down the sides of the bottle gradually until it covers the fruit.

Twist the bottle from side to side and gently agitate as you add the syrup or water to remove any air bubbles.

Slow Water Bath Method

The benefit of this method is that fruits do not tend to float to the top of the jar and it is actually quite energy efficient. It does take some skill and practice to get the timing right though. A thermometer is really required for this and you might like to have a trial run with a pan full of water to get some idea before you start for real.

The fruit is packed into jars and cold syrup is poured over, as described above. Put the lids onto the jars and then place on a rack or trivet in the bottom of the pan, ensuring there is a little space between the jars.

Cover with cold water and then put a lid onto the pan. Gently heat the water so that it reaches a temperature of 55°C (130°F) for over an hour. It has to be gentle heat so that we're sure the contents of the jar have reached the same temperature as the water.

Now turn the heat up a little and bring it up to the recommended temperature over the next half hour. If you don't have a thermometer this is difficult to measure so bring to simmering point, approximately 90°C (195°F) or use that to try and gauge the temperature.

Once at the correct temperature, hold for the required time (see chart on page 43) and then remove the jars to a cooling rack, leaving space between the jars for airflow. Check and tighten the lids. Allow to cool and then label with contents and date before storing in a cool, dark place. Although the produce will store well, light can cause discoloration. One day someone may start selling dark glass preserving jars – buy them!

The next day when the jars are at room temperature, double-check that the seal on the lids is tight. The way to do this is to carefully undo the clips or unscrew ring sealed jars and then gently lift by the lid. If there is a good seal, the lid will stay on due to the vacuum in the jar.

Where you are using the thin metal lids, check if the centre of the lid can be depressed. If it is flexible, then it has not sealed correctly.

With metal screw rings, a rub over with a little Vaseline will prevent corrosion and ensure it unscrews easily after months on the shelf.

If the seal is broken, you can re-process the fruit and syrup separately but be aware the quality will not be so good. Alternatively, place in the fridge for use over the next couple of days.

Fast Water Bath Method

This is cheating a little to reduce time and energy use but you may have problems with loosely packed fruits rising in the jar.

Pack the jars but add hot syrup, ideally at 60°C (140°F) to the fruit. Place in the pan as before and cover in warm water (around 40°C/104°F). Once again your thermometer comes in handy. If you don't have one, then use your judgement; 40°C is just a little over blood heat.

Bring the temperature up to simmering point over half an hour and then hold as per the chart on page 44. After this time, treat exactly as the slow water bath method processed fruit.

Water Bath Bottling Charts

Bring to simmering temperature as described above and then hold for the time listed. Timings are based on jars up to 1 quart (1 litre) size.

Slow Water Bath Method

Fruit	Ideal Temp.	Time (mins.)
Apples – in Syrup	74°C/165°F	10
Apples – Solid Pack	82°C/180°F	15
Apricots	82°C/180°F	15
Blackberries/Loganberries/ Raspberries	74°C/165°F	10
Cherries	82°C/180°F	15
Citrus Fruits – Orange, Lemon, Grapefruit, etc.	82°C/180°F	15
Currants – Black, Red or White	74°C/165°F	10
Gooseberries – for cooking in pies, etc.	74°C/165°F	10
Gooseberries – for uncooked use in desserts	82°C/180°F	15
Peaches	82°C/180°F	15
Pears	88°C/190°F	30
Pineapple	82°C/180°F	15
Plums and Damsons	82°C/180°F	15
Rhubarb – for cooking in pies, etc.	74°C/165°F	10
Rhubarb – for uncooked use in desserts	82°C/180°F	15
Strawberries – in Syrup	82°C/180°F	15
Tomatoes – Solid pack	88°C/190°F	40
Tomatoes – in Brine	88°C/190°F	30

Fast Water Bath Method

If you don't have a thermometer, this method is preferable as the ideal temperature is 88°C (190°F) which is just about the temperature of a slow simmer and easy to judge by eye.

Fruit	Time (mins.)
Apples – in Syrup	2
Apples – Solid Pack	20
Apricots	10
Blackberries/Loganberries/Raspberries	2
Cherries	10
Citrus Fruits – Orange, Lemon, Grapefruit, etc.	10
Currants – Black, Red or White	10
Gooseberries – for cooking in pies, etc.	2
Gooseberries – for uncooked use in desserts	10
Peaches	20
Pears	40
Pineapple	20
Plums and Damsons	10
Rhubarb – for cooking in pies, etc.	2
Rhubarb – for uncooked use in desserts	10
Strawberries	2
Tomatoes – Solid pack	40
Tomatoes – in Brine	50

Oven – Dry Pack

This method is not suitable for light-coloured fruits which discolour in air like apples, pears, peaches, apricots, etc., or for solid pack tomatoes. It is quite straightforward though.

Pre-heat the oven to Gas Mark ½ (120°C, 250°F). Pack the bottles with the fruit but do not pour over the syrup or liquid at this stage. Place the lids on top but without the clips or screw bands.

Put the bottles onto a baking tray in the centre of the oven, allowing at least 2 inches (50 mm) between each bottle and the sides of the oven. Leave for the amount of time indicated on the chart on page 46. To be successful with this method you have to be quick when filling and sealing the bottles – do this as soon as they are removed from the oven.

After the processing, remove the bottles one at a time and fill quickly to the top with boiling syrup or water, securing the lids with clips or screw-bands immediately. If the fruit has shrunk down in the bottles, add fruit from another bottle before pouring over the syrup or water. Leave for 24 hours and test for seal.

Oven – Wet Pack

This method can be used for all types of fruit and also for solid pack tomatoes.

Pre-heat the oven to Gas Mark 2 (150°C, 300°F). Pack warm bottles with the fruit and poor in boiling syrup, brine or water allowing 1 inch (25 mm) headroom.

Place the lids on top but not the clips or screw bands. Put the bottles 2 inches (50 mm) apart on a baking tray with a lip in case any liquid boils out during processing, on the centre shelf of the oven.

After the processing time, given in the chart below, remove the bottles one at a time and secure the lids with clips or screw bands. Leave for 24 hours and test for seal.

Oven Bottling Chart

Timings are based on jars up to 1 quart (1 litre) size. NR = Not Recommended

Fruit	Wet Pack (mins.)	Dry Pack (mins.)
Apples – in Syrup	30–40	NR
Apples – Solid Pack	50–60	NR
Apricots	40–50	NR
Blackberries/Loganberries/ Raspberries	30–40	45–55
Cherries	40–50	55–70
Citrus Fruits – Orange, Lemon, Grapefruit, etc.	40–50	NR
Currants – Black, Red or White	40–50	55–70
Gooseberries – for cooking in pies, etc.	30–40	45–55
Gooseberries – for uncooked use in desserts	40–50	55–70
Peaches	50–60	NR
Pears	60–70	NR
Pineapple	50–60	NR
Plums and Damsons	45–60	NR
Rhubarb – for cooking in pies, etc.	30–40	45–55
Rhubarb – for uncooked use in desserts	40–50	55–70
Strawberries	50–60	NR
Tomatoes – Solid pack	70–80	NR
Tomatoes – in Brine	60–70	80–100

Pressure Bottling

Bottling under pressure is the most energy efficient method as raising the pressure increases the boiling point of water and thereby the temperature that the food is processed at, so reducing the amount of time taken.

Purpose-made pressure canners are very difficult to find in Britain – we only found one very expensive model – but they are easily available (and at much lower prices) in the USA. Pressure canners tend to be a larger capacity than pressure cookers, which probably accounts for the price difference. Accordingly, our instructions are based on using an ordinary pressure cooker. It must, obviously, be deep enough for your jars including a trivet on the bottom to prevent direct heat cracking the jars. We use a hi-dome cooker which allows plenty of headroom.

The drawback of pressure bottling is that you are limited to how many jars you can fit in your pressure cooker at one time.

For bottling vegetables with low acid content, pressure bottling is the only safe route as the botulism bacterium can survive boiling water. The higher boiling point temperature for the period given guarantees that the bacteria are dead.

The method is simple enough. Pack the fruit or vegetables into hot jars and then fill with boiling syrup or brine for vegetables. Loosely fix the lids onto the jars. Whilst filling your jars, heat about 850 ml of water (1½ Imp pints, 1.8 US pints) in the pressure cooker to near boiling and then place your jars in, ensuring they are sitting on a trivet so not subjected to direct heat and not touching each other.

Place the lid on the cooker and bring to operating temperature. For high acid fruits, cook on the L weight setting, 5 lb, **but low acid vegetables must be processed on the M weight setting, 10 lb.**

Different cookers have different methods so check your manual. With ours we allow the steam to escape for 5 minutes before placing the weights on but more modern ones have this purging automatically handled by the safety release valve.

Cook for the time given at pressure and then remove from the heat. Allow the cooker to cool naturally. Don't pour cold water over it to hurry the process. Once cool enough to have reduced the pressure inside, you can remove the lid and take the bottles out onto a cooling rack. Tighten the seals if necessary.

One word of warning: if you're not used to pressure cooking, double check that the pressure has abated by gently lifting the weights. On our old model it is possible to unlock the lid whilst at pressure. The effect of doing that would literally be a small explosion of super-heated steam and water which could have awful results.

Double check the seals on the jars of processed fruit with the lifting test the next day as for other methods.

Timing Chart for Pressure Bottling Fruit

Time begins once pressure (L or 5 lb) has been attained and the heat has been reduced to prevent over-steaming.

Fruit	Time (mins.)
Apples – in Syrup	1
Apples – Solid Pack	3–4
Apricots	1
Blackberries/Loganberries/Raspberries	1
Cherries	1
Citrus Fruits – Orange, Lemon, Grapefruit, etc., in syrup	1
Currants – Black, Red or White	1
Gooseberries – for cooking in pies, etc.	1
Gooseberries – for uncooked use in desserts	1
Peaches	3–4
Pears	5
Pineapple	3
Plums and Damsons	1
Rhubarb – for cooking in pies, etc.	1
Rhubarb – for uncooked use in desserts	1
Strawberries	1
Tomatoes – Solid pack	15
Tomatoes – in Brine	5

Timing Chart for Pressure Bottling Vegetables

Time begins once pressure (M or 10 lb) has been attained and the heat has been reduced to prevent over-steaming.

Vegetable	Blanching Time (mins.)	Time at Pressure (mins.)
Asparagus	2–3	35
Broad (Fava) Beans	3	40
French & Runner Beans	3	35
Peas	2	45
Sweet Peppers	3–5	40
Sweetcorn (blanch on the cob)	6	50
Low Acid Tomatoes – Solid pack	N/A	25
Low Acid Tomatoes – in Brine	N/A	20

Bottled Apple or Pear Juice

Taste the juice as each batch will vary according to the type of apples and time harvested. You may wish to add a little sugar or honey if it's too tart for you. With apple juice, a little cinnamon can really pep up the flavour. Heat your apple juice in a pan until it is just below simmering point and then pour into sterilized storage jars, leaving just a little headroom, ¼ inch or 5 mm.

Put the lid on and place into a bath of boiling water. It's easiest to have the pan half full of boiling water as you add the jars and then top up from another pan of boiling water so the jars are covered by an inch or two (25–50 mm) of water.

Boil for 5 minutes, remove the jars from the pan, cool and tighten the tops if necessary. After 24 hours check the seals as for bottled fruits.

Elevation

As we explained in pressure bottling, water boils at different temperatures according to the air pressure. This is a problem often encountered by mountaineers. They can boil water at a low temperature so they can't actually cook things or get a decent cup of tea in the rarefied low pressure air.

If you happen to live at high level, then you need to take this into account when bottling. The formula below gives compensation timings and pressures for different elevations above sea level.

For every 1,000 feet or 300 metres above sea level you need to add the following:

- For boiling times below 20 minutes, add 1 minute
- For boiling times above 20 minutes, add 2 minutes
- For pressure bottling add ½ lb pressure per 1,000 feet, 300 metres. If bottling vegetables and you cannot control the pressure accurately, use the H, 15 lb weight setting to be safe.

8
Chutneys

●

The heyday of chutney was undoubtedly the Victorian era. Unlike today, where we treat chutney as a condiment, complementing a meal, in those days chutney was a method of preserving foods for use the year round and formed a major part of a meal.

The name chutney derives from the Hindi word, Chatni, as the method and spices originally came from India. These were imported into Britain during the days of the Raj and soon became as British as our national dish of Chicken Tikka Massala.

Chutneys are made from fruits or vegetables, or a mixture of the two, which are chopped, cooked, mixed with spices, vinegar and other ingredients and reduced to a smooth pulp.

There are literally hundreds of recipes for chutney, or you can make up your own once you have the method understood. They can be primarily sweet or sour, hot as Hades using lots of chilli peppers or quite mild. You're not limited to fixed recipes with chutney; if you are short on one ingredient then substitute another.

Unlike other storage methods where you really want the best quality produce, with chutney you can use damaged fruits, end of season produce, etc. – a great way to turn second-class produce into a first-class product.

Chutneys store really well. We have perfectly edible chutney in the store cupboard that's over three years old. In fact, it usually takes a chutney at least three months to develop its final flavour and it continues to improve with age. However, in this age of litigation, we are told it is wise not to suggest you keep your chutney over a year. Personally we've enjoyed chutneys made three years ago and we're still here to write about it.

As with any homemade food product, do use your common sense. If it smells or tastes off, then don't take the risk of eating it. We even had an email asking if chutney with mould growing on it was safe to eat once. Common sense isn't as common as it should be.

Chutneys store well as they use a combination of methods to remove any microbes and prevent them growing. First there is the long cooking which pretty well sterilizes the chutney. Then there is the sugar content that causes osmotic disruption of any microbes. In effect the sugar sucks the moisture out of their cells by osmosis, thereby killing any microbes. Next we have the acidity caused by the vinegar and finally we have the anti-septic properties of some of the spices and ingredients like garlic and chilli.

However, this multi-layered protection is no reason not to be scrupulous about hygiene and sterilization when making chutneys.

Equipment for Making Chutney

You can probably find all the equipment you need to make chutney in the kitchen already.

A **large pan** is a must. This should be either stainless steel or enamel lined. Do not use brass, copper or iron pans as they may react with the vinegar and add a metallic flavour to your chutney.

A long-handled wooden or stainless steel **spoon** for stirring is needed but if you use a wooden spoon it will tend to absorb the spicy flavours so we'd recommend keeping it just for chutney making.

You'll also need **muslin or cotton squares** to tie up whole spices, which are needed for a lot of recipes. Plus **scales** for weighing ingredients, and a **slotted spoon** for removing spice bags, etc.

To store your chutney you will need **heat-proof glass jars**. Kilner or Mason style are ideal with the glass lids or you can save up jars from commercial pickles, etc., so long as the glass is suitable and, most

importantly, the lid. Vinegar corrodes metal so metal lids should be the plastic-coated type.

Your friends and neighbours will be a good source for jars. Swap a jar of your produce for a box of empty jars with them. You'll be surprised how they remember to save them up for you.

Finally, once you've made your chutney you'll need labels. We use ordinary printer labels designed for parcels and then we use the computer to create fancy designs. All that's really important is the contents and date, but a fancy label turns them into an ideal gift or swap item.

Ingredients

As we said above, you can use damaged or misshaped fruits and vegetables in your chutney. You'll be adding vinegar, sugar and spices to these and the vinegar is critical to successful storage. It doesn't matter whether you use malt, wine or white vinegar so long as the acetic acid content is over 5 per cent. This is usually marked on the bottle. If not, assume the acid content is low and buy another brand. A chutney made with low-acid vinegar is certainly not going to store as well as that made with high-acid vinegars and the flavour will lack the sharpness a good vinegar imparts.

The sugar in chutney can be ordinary white or brown and some recipes use molasses which can be substituted with brown sugar or vice versa. Brown sugar is going to produce a darker chutney than white but prolonged cooking has a darkening effect on chutney anyway. So if you want a light-coloured chutney, use white sugar and add it towards the end of the cooking process when the fruit and vegetables are already well softened.

Often you will use whole spices in a muslin bag for chutney which gives it a brighter final appearance. Bruise the spices before tying into a muslin bag which is removed from the pan after cooking. You'll find that many recipes call for a mixture of whole and ground spice though. If you have dried spices that have been at the back of the shelf for years (it happens to us all) do watch out that the flavour hasn't evaporated. Your nose should tell you.

Tasting is a very rough guide when you make chutneys. As we said, it takes a few months for flavours to integrate and mature. However, with practice you'll be able to make a fair estimate of how the finished product is going to taste from the cooking chutney.

Don't be afraid to alter recipes. Generally keep the proportions of vegetables/fruit to sugar and vinegar the same but you may substitute similar vegetables or fruit and add or subtract from spices. For example, if you like things hot then add more hot spices like chilli pepper. You make your chutney to suit yourself and your family's tastes, not some focus group of average shoppers. That's why it's better.

Do not substitute artificial sweetener for sugar. The sugar is there as much as a preservative as for the sweetness, and artificial sweetener will not do the job.

Sterilizing Jars

If you have an automatic dishwasher, then we'd recommend putting the jars and lids through on the hottest wash available. Some dishwashers actually incorporate a sterilize program.

Otherwise wash thoroughly in hot soapy water, rinse well in hot water and allow to drain. When you start cooking the chutney, pop the jars and lids into a low oven, Gas Mark 1 (140°C/275°F). Be careful when you remove them – they will be hot.

Green Tomato Chutney

Makes about 3 kg (6½ lb) of chutney

A traditional chutney for using up surplus green tomatoes.
Makes a good "cook in" sauce for chicken, as an accompaniment for curry
and is excellent on a cheese sandwich.

2.25 kg (5 lb) green tomatoes
500 g (1 lb)onions
25 g (1 oz) salt
250 g (8 oz) seedless raisins
250 g (8 oz) sultanas
25 g (1 oz) root ginger
4 red chillies (see page 151)
1 tablespoon whole black peppercorns
12 cloves
500 g (1 lb 2 oz) demerara sugar
600 ml (21 fluid oz) malt vinegar

1. Wash and finely chop the tomatoes. Peel and finely chop the onions.
2. Place the two together in a bowl, sprinkle with the salt and leave for at least an hour.
3. Transfer into a pan with the raisins and sultanas. Bruise the ginger and chillies and put with the other spices into a piece of muslin, tie firmly and add to the pan with the vinegar.
4. Bring to the boil and then switch down to a simmer, add the sugar stirring frequently until dissolved.
5. Continue stirring occasionally and press onto the muslin bag until thickened.
6. Remove the muslin bag.
7. Pour into hot sterilized jars and seal.

Never add hot chutney to a cold jar. The thermal shock can crack the glass or in the worst case cause it to shatter.

When things go Wrong

We hate those books that tell you how to do something and assume you'll get a perfect result every time. Life isn't quite that neat!

When you follow a recipe, stick to the same measuring system throughout. Don't mix US, UK and metric amounts. Even if two options are shown, follow only one. We adjust our recipes to make them easier, rounding up ingredients, etc.

If you decide to make smaller or larger quantities, double check your maths and write down the recipe. The number of people we speak to who doubled the fruit, doubled the sugar but, for example, forgot to double the vinegar is surprising.

Undercooking is a common problem. You think the chutney is done and pour into jars only to notice that liquid has risen to the top after a short time. You can rescue this, pour the chutney back into the pan and simmer to drive off the excess juice. While you're re-cooking, wash and re-sterilize the jars (don't miss this step).

If the chutney has been in the jar for a month or so and you notice the level has dropped, then the lid was loose and moisture has evaporated. Check that all the other lids are on tight. The chutney may be all right, but if mould has started, throw it away. It's annoying, but not as bad as food poisoning.

Taste the chutney. If you try it and it's too sweet or too vinegary, don't despair. Often it's just a matter of allowing time for the flavours to mature. It's very much like a young wine – harsh and acid – that a year later is a smooth delight.

Recipes

We've covered making chutney in more detail in our book *Easy Jams, Preserves and Chutneys* with a host of recipes and you can find quite a few on our website www.allotment.org.uk/recipe or the internet generally. The recipes in this chapter will give you a good idea of the general principles and method.

Hot Aubergine (Eggplant) Chutney

Makes about 1.5 kg (3 lb) of chutney

A hot and tasty way for preserving aubergines (eggplants)
over the winter months. Delicious with cheese.

1 kg (2 lb) aubergines (eggplants)
3 tablespoons salt
175 g (6 oz) soft dark brown sugar
350 ml (12 fl oz) white wine vinegar
75 g (3 oz) seedless raisins or sultanas
1 tablespoon tomato purée
500 g (1 lb) onions
3 red chillies
5 cloves of garlic (crushed)
1 teaspoon cayenne pepper

1. Slice the aubergines, put into a colander and sprinkle with the salt. Leave for at least three hours, then rinse and dry.
2. Meanwhile, put the sugar, vinegar, raisins or sultanas and tomato purée into a bowl, mix and leave to stand.
3. Finely chop the onions and red chillies (watch your eyes – see page 151) and place with all of the other ingredients into a pan.
4. Heat gently, stirring until the sugar is dissolved, then simmer until thickened.
5. Pour into hot sterilized jars and seal.

Apple Chutney

Makes about 2 kg (4 lb) of chutney

A simple chutney that is easy to make but nobody
will believe that when they taste it.

1 kg (2 lb) cooking apples
250 g (8 oz) onions
250 g (8 oz) raisins or sultanas
15 g (½ oz) salt
1 litre (35 fl oz) white wine vinegar
60 g (2 oz) mixed pickling spice
2 teaspoons ground ginger
500 g (1 lb) brown sugar

1. Peel, core and slice the apples. Peel and chop the onions.
2. Put the onions, apples, raisins or sultanas, and salt into a pan with the vinegar. Tie the pickling spice in a muslin bag and add to the pan. Bring to the boil, then reduce the heat and simmer until tender. Remove the spice and add the ginger.
3. Add the sugar, stir until it has dissolved. Bring to the boil. Boil until the chutney is thick.
4. Pot into hot, clean, sterilized jars immediately and seal.
5. Label with contents once fully cooled.

Mixed Fruit Chutney

Makes about 1.5 kg (3 lb) of chutney

No two batches of this chutney are ever exactly the same.
The flavour changes a little every time as different types
of fruit in different proportions are used.

500 g (1 lb) onions
1.5 kg (3 lb) mixed fruit – apples, pears, plums, damsons, etc.
120 g (4 oz) dried dates
2 cloves of garlic
1 teaspoon salt
1 teaspoon mixed spice
1 teaspoon dry mustard
500 g (1 lb) soft brown sugar
600 ml (20 fl oz) vinegar

1. Peel and chop the onions and boil in a little water until they are soft. Drain.
2. Wash, peel and core the fruits and chop into pieces. Chop the dates. Crush the garlic.
3. Put all the ingredients into a pan, bring to the boil, then reduce the heat and simmer, stirring frequently until the chutney is thick.
4. Ladle into hot, clean, sterilized jars, cover and seal.

Courgette Chutney

Makes about 2 kg (4 lb) of chutney

A good way to use up some of those surplus courgettes,
and a must with a chunk of really sharp cheese.

1.5 kg (3 lb) courgettes
Salt
250 g (8 oz) cooking apples
250 g (8 oz) shallots
250 g (8 oz) sultanas
120 g (4 oz) brown sugar
600 ml (20 fl oz) vinegar
15 g (½ oz) bruised root ginger
2 teaspoons pickling spice

1. Peel the courgettes if the skin is tough and dice into cubes.
    Put in layers in a bowl with a generous sprinkling of salt.
    Leave overnight.
2. Drain, rinse thoroughly and put into a pan.
3. Peel and chop the apples and shallots and add to the
    courgettes with the sultanas, sugar, vinegar and spices (tied
    in a piece of muslin).
4. Bring to the boil very slowly and then simmer gently until
    cooked and thick.
5. Pour into hot, clean, sterilized jars and seal at once.
6. Label with contents when fully cooled.

Mixed Mushroom Chutney

Makes about 2 kg (4 lb) of chutney

You can use field or button mushrooms, cutting the first into small chunks
or leaving small button mushrooms whole for a different texture.

1 largish red pepper
250 g (8 oz) onions
500 g (1 lb) cooking apples
500 g (1 lb) mushrooms
250 g (8 oz) red tomatoes
60 g (2 oz) root ginger
500 g (1 lb) brown sugar
250 g (8 oz) raisins or sultanas
600 ml (20 fl oz) vinegar

1. De-seed the pepper and chop finely. Peel and chop the onions. Put into a pan with about 300 ml (10 fl oz) water. Simmer to soften.
2. Peel, core and chop the apples. Wash and coarsely chop the mushrooms. Skin and chop the tomatoes.
3. Add the apples, mushrooms and tomatoes to the pepper and onion and continue cooking.
4. Grate the root ginger and add to the pan. Simmer until tender.
5. Add the sugar, raisins or sultanas and vinegar and stir until the sugar has dissolved.
6. Bring to the boil and then reduce to a simmer and stir occasionally to prevent sticking.
7. Continue to simmer until all the liquid is absorbed and the chutney is thick.
8. Pot into hot, clean, sterilized jars immediately and seal.

Mango Chutney

Makes about 1.5 kg (3 lb) of chutney

Although we don't grow mangoes in the UK as they're a tropical fruit, we do eat a lot of chutney. This one is a must with a super hot curry where the sweetness gives some respite when your mouth is on fire!

1 kg (2 lb) mangoes
1 tablespoon salt
500 g (1 lb) onions
60 g (2 oz) root ginger
4–6 cloves garlic
5 cm (2 inch) stick of cinnamon
180 g (6 oz) raisins
2 teaspoons hot chilli powder
1 tablespoon mustard seeds
1 litre (35 fl oz) distilled malt (white) vinegar
500 g (1 lb) soft brown sugar

1. Peel, halve and remove the stones from the mangoes and cut into small slices. Layer in a bowl, sprinkle with the salt and leave to steep overnight.
2. Rinse and drain the mangoes. Peel and finely chop the onions. Peel and finely chop the root ginger. Peel and chop the garlic. Tie the stick of cinnamon in a muslin bag.
3. Put all the ingredients except the sugar into a pan with the vinegar. Bring to the boil and simmer until soft.
4. Add the sugar and stir until it has dissolved. Continue simmering until the chutney thickens, stirring occasionally.
5. Remove the cinnamon stick and pour into hot sterilized jars and seal.

9
Ketchups and Sauces

●

The range of sauces and ketchups on the supermarket shelves can all be duplicated at home, with the added benefit that you can create the flavour you and your family find most appealing. The prime example of this has to be the most popular sauce (in the UK at least) of tomato ketchup. It's very popular with children, being sweet, but lacks a bite that would make it more of a grown-up accompaniment.

The process of making sauces is similar in some ways to that of making a chutney, in that you cook the ingredients together and bottle them but they then require secondary sterilization in a water bath in just the same way as bottled fruits are processed to store safely.

Equipment

For the processing you require the same range of equipment as for making chutney and for bottling. Usually sauces go into narrow-necked bottles, although you can use wide-necked preserving jars. The glass in the bottles needs to be thick enough to cope with the sterilizing process and you need to be able to seal the bottle afterwards.

Corks are commonly used, but corks are slightly porous so, once the bottle is corked, seal the exposed end either with candle wax or with those plastic wine sheaves that shrink on when heated with a

Plum Ketchup

Makes about 1.2 litres (2 Imp pints, 2½ US pints) of ketchup

This light brown, spicy sauce will brighten up a range of dishes. Despite plums being the main ingredient, this is a savoury ketchup, not a dessert sauce.

2 kg (4 lb) plums
250 g (8 oz) onions
125 g (4 oz) currants
4 chillies (see page 151)
2 thumb-sized pieces of root ginger
1 teaspoon black peppercorns
1 teaspoon whole allspice
600 ml (18 Imp fl oz, 17 US fl oz) malt vinegar
250 g (8 oz) sugar
2 teaspoons salt

1. Quarter the plums and remove the stones, peel and dice the onions.
2. Place all the ingredients except the sugar, salt and half the vinegar in a pan and simmer for 30 minutes stirring to prevent sticking.
3. Rub through a sieve and return to the pan.
4. Add the sugar, salt and remaining vinegar, then simmer for an hour or so until thickened.
5. Pour into sterilized bottles and seal.
6. Process in a water bath, simmering at around 88°C (190°F) for 10 minutes.

hair-dryer. Always use new corks and boil them for ten minutes before using to sterilize and soften them.

You can also buy preserving bottles with a clip-on lid in the UK, similar to those used by some German beer companies. In the US you can buy specific canning bottles with a screw-on lid.

If you are using jars, then use a smaller size as the contents will only keep for about three to four weeks when the jar is opened. Store in a refrigerator when opened.

Basic Tomato Ketchup

This recipe is quite similar to the store-bought versions but think of it as a basis for your own recipe. Changing from a basic distilled malt vinegar to a wine vinegar (do check that it's 5 per cent or greater acid content though), adding cloves, adding nutmeg or increasing the pepper will all affect the eventual result.

Don't forget that the main ingredient, tomatoes, will vary as well. The variety grown is just one factor, how they are grown also makes a difference. Forced, hothouse tomatoes tend to be weaker in flavour than those grown outdoors under a hot sun. The water content will vary as well along with the ripeness, depending when picked.

All these variations present a problem for commercial manufacturers who seek a consistent product but add to the charm of homemade. Just as cheap, blended wines are consistent year on year but the really great wines vary vintage on vintage, your homemade products will be good one year but absolutely fantastic the next.

One way we've found to cope with watery tomatoes, besides cooking for longer, is to concentrate the flavour by partially drying some of them which adds depth to the flavour.

Cut your tomatoes in half and lay on a baking tray in the oven, cut side up. Put the oven on its lowest setting (Gas Mark 1 or 100°C, 212°F) and leave for about 2 to 3 hours. Smaller tomatoes will dry faster than large ones, so keep an eye on them. Fully dried, equivalent to the sun-dried tomatoes you can buy, takes between 6 and 12 hours but you just want to concentrate the flavour and get them to start to shrivel.

Basic Tomato Ketchup

Makes about 1.2 litres (2 Imp pints, 2½ US pints) of ketchup

3 kg (6½ lb) ripe red tomatoes
1 teaspoon celery salt
1 tablespoon salt
250 g (8 or 9 oz) granulated sugar
2 teaspoons paprika
Pinch of cayenne pepper
300 ml (10 fl oz) distilled (white) malt vinegar

1. Wash the tomatoes and chop them. There's no need to skin or remove the seeds.
2. Put in a pan and heat slowly until pulped, stirring occasionally.
3. Press through a sieve and return the purée to a clean pan.
4. Add the remaining ingredients and stir until the sugar has dissolved.
5. Bring to the boil and then reduce the heat and simmer gently until the sauce has thickened.
6. Pour into hot, sterilized bottles and seal.
7. Process using a fast hot water bath (see page 42) ideally raising the temperature to 77°C (170°F) for 30 minutes. If you don't have a thermometer, at this temperature you should see a small amount of bubbles raising from the bottom of the pan but not enough to call the water boiling.

10
Pickles

●

Pickling is another time-honoured method of storage relying on the acidity of the vinegar to preserve the produce. Pickles range from the simple one ingredient to complex condiments shading into chutneys.

The critical item is the vinegar. It must have an acetic acid content of 5 per cent or higher to work. You can buy readymade pickling vinegar or make your own by steeping bruised spices tied in a muslin bag in the vinegar for six to eight weeks. If you are pressed for time, here is a quick method.

Put the vinegar and spice bag into a covered bowl and stand on a saucepan of water. Bring the water to the boil so the steam very gently warms the vinegar and then leave for 3 hours to allow the flavours to infuse. If you can leave it for longer, do so.

Making your own pickling vinegar keeps you in the driving seat. For something like pickled eggs you can make a mildly spiced vinegar but for onions you can go as wild and hot as you will with the spices. Some common mixes are detailed on the next page.

Pickled Eggs

These are a traditional favourite in pubs and chip shops, yet so easy to make at home and a great way to store a summer glut of eggs.

Mild Spiced Vinegar

5 g (1 tsp) cinnamon
5 g (1 tsp) cloves
5 g (1 tsp) mace
5 g (1 tsp) whole pimento (allspice)
6 peppercorns

Medium Spiced Vinegar

5 g (1 tsp) cinnamon
5 g (1 tsp) cloves
5 g (1 tsp) white peppercorns
5 g (1 tsp) dried root ginger
5 g (1 tsp) mace
5 g (1 tsp) pimento (allspice)

Hot Spiced Vinegar

30 g (1 oz) mustard seeds
10 g (2 tsp) dried chillies
15 g (3 tsp) cloves
15 g (3 tsp) black peppercorns
30 g (1 oz) pimento (allspice)

*Each of these provides sufficient spices for 1 litre, 1.8 Imp pints
or 2.1 US pints of vinegar.*

You need wide-necked sealable jars – 1 quart Mason jars or 1 litre Kilner jars are ideal.

The best eggs for this are about two weeks old, so they're easier to peel. To hard boil the eggs place into a saucepan of cool water and then bring to the boil, stirring the eggs gently during the first few minutes of boiling. This helps ensure that the yolks are centralized.

Boil for about 8 to 10 minutes and then plunge into cold water immediately to prevent the yolks getting a black ring around them. Peel the eggs and put into your oven-sterilized jar whilst heating the vinegar in a saucepan. You don't want to boil the vinegar, but you do want it hot. The best pickling vinegar for eggs is the mild spiced vinegar. Try doubling the amount of cloves in the standard recipe; it works well with eggs.

Pour the hot vinegar into the jar over the eggs and seal the jars, label and store. Allow three weeks for the vinegar flavour to permeate the eggs.

Pickled Onions

Another traditional favourite, pickled onions really need a good strong cheese, crusty bread and a strong ale to help them down.
You can use special pickling varieties of onion or ordinary onions grown closely together to keep them dwarf or shallots if you wish.

1.5 litres (2½ Imp pints, 3 US pints) water
500 g (1 lb) salt
1.5 kg (3 lb) pickling onions or shallots
Approx 600 ml (1 Imp pint, 1.2 US pints) Hot Spiced Vinegar

1. Make a brine by boiling the water and salt together in a pan until all the salt has dissolved. Leave until quite cold before using.
2. Put the unpeeled onions into the brine and soak overnight – using a plate or something similar to keep the onions below the surface of the brine.
3. Drain and peel and then put back in some fresh brine and soak again for a day or two.
4. Rinse well.
5. Pack into clean, sterilized jars and cover with cold Hot Spiced Vinegar.
6. Cover and label with contents and date.

Pickled Red Cabbage

You can use the same recipe for Pickled White Cabbage.

Red cabbage
Salt
Spiced vinegar

1. Cut off and discard the outer discoloured leaves from the cabbage.
2. Quarter and remove the tough inner stalk. Shred the cabbage, wash and drain well.
3. Layer in a basin with salt between layers, ending with a layer of salt.
4. Leave for 24 hours.
5. Wash thoroughly in cold water and drain well.
6. Pack into clean, sterilized jars and pour in cold, spiced vinegar.
7. Cover the jars and label with contents and date.

It's ready after one week but if you keep it longer than 10–12 weeks it will lose its crispness.

Pickled Beetroot

Beetroot
Water
Spiced vinegar

1. Wash the beetroot carefully without rubbing the skin.
2. Cook gently in a large pan, covering the beetroot with water, until tender (the length of time will depend on the size of the beetroot).
3. Allow to cool and then rub off the skins.
4. Large beetroot can be cut into slices of about 0.5 cm (¼ inch) or diced into cubes.
5. Pack into clean, sterilized, jars and cover with cold spiced vinegar.
6. Seal and label with date and contents.

You can use boiling spiced vinegar instead – this makes the storage life longer and it retains the colour.

Pickled Mushrooms

Mushrooms
Salt
Spiced vinegar

1. Choose small mushrooms if you can. Otherwise cut larger ones into half or quarters. Wash the mushrooms and wipe dry.
2. Layer with salt in a basin, finishing with a layer of salt.
3. Leave for several hours, stirring occasionally.
4. When the liquor has emerged from the mushrooms, pack into clean, sterilized jars with a little of the liquor and cover with cold spiced vinegar.
5. Cover and label with contents and date.

This is best if left for at least two weeks before using.

Pickled Cucumber

Cucumbers
Salt
Spiced vinegar

1. Wash the cucumbers and wipe clean. Do not peel unless they are bitter.
2. Cut into slices or dice into cubes.
3. Layer with salt in a basin, finishing with a layer of salt.
4. Leave for 24 hours.
5. Rinse thoroughly in cold water and drain well.
6. Pack into clean, sterilized jars and cover with cold spiced vinegar.
7. Cover and label with contents and date.

This is best if left for 4 weeks before using.

11

Jams, Jellies and Marmalades

●

omemade jam is enjoying a bit of a resurgence nowadays, although jams as a shop product are not as popular as they once were. The reasons that jam has generally lost favour are twofold. Firstly, the endless pressure to be cheaper is achieved by sacrificing quality, which means that store-bought jams just aren't as good as they once were, unless you pay a small fortune for artisan or premium brands.

Secondly, sugar has become demonized and jams contain a lot of sugar. Sugar itself isn't bad for you, but large quantities of sugar in your diet aren't a good thing. The main culprit for sugar in the diet is processed foods where it sneaks in without you even realizing it. Checking a popular brand of baked beans reveals that 5 per cent of the content is sugar. So we contend that eating a healthy diet of home-grown and produced real foods leaves room for a treat that is high in sugar.

You can make low-sugar jams, but these aren't really jams that will sit in the store cupboard. They have very short shelf lives and need refrigerating to manage that. If you're worried about sugar, check the labels on any processed food to see the amount in there before feeling guilty about your jam.

Jams and marmalades are an effective way to store summer fruit gluts. The high-sugar content causes osmotic disruption in bacteria and microbes which is a fancy way of saying it sucks the moisture out of them. Just place a sugar cube in a small puddle of water to see it in action. The boiling sterilizes the contents and so long as the lids are on firmly and airtight, your jams will keep well for at least a year.

Incidentally, if you have fruit such as strawberries that arrive over a period of time in season, just keep freezing the surplus until you have enough for a jam-making session.

Jams are extremely versatile and have many uses beyond accompanying bread and butter or toast. They can be used in homemade scones, pancakes, fillings for sponge cakes, biscuits, steamed puddings, baked puddings, trifles and ice-cream to name a few.

Equipment for Jam Making

You have probably all you need for jam making already in the kitchen. A large saucepan will suffice but a good quality preserving pan makes the process easier.

If you move onto jellies and marmalades, a straining bag and support for it will be needed. You can get specialist jam thermometers quite cheaply. We managed for years without one and can't really say we use the one we finally bought. Still, if you think it helps, they're not expensive.

One tool we have found really useful is a non-stick wide-necked jam funnel. No more runs of jam on the outside of the jar.

These are available from specialist suppliers. If your local stores can't help, there are many suppliers on the internet.

Not really equipment but not an ingredient either is a bottle of methylated spirits. This is used to determine if the jam will set (see below) and to shine up the outside of the jars, removing old label residue, etc.

The only other items you will need are jam jars. You can buy new ones, but we just re-use commercial jars given to us by friends and neighbours. Wash them thoroughly when you get them and discard any with chips in them.

Ingredients

The fruit should be of good quality, preferably a little under ripe rather than over ripe as under ripe fruits tend to contain more pectin which is needed for setting. Avoid mouldy fruit — it's asking for trouble — and ensure that the fruit is dry before you start. Wet fruit encourages mould.

There's a lot of confusion over sugar for jam making. We hardly ever use special sugar. Ordinary white granulated is perfectly adequate and the cheapest. If you are making a lot of jam, do check if the store sells large bags at a discount. We found that 8 kg catering bags save us a little money on the standard 1 kg bag.

You can buy special preserving sugar which is supposed to reduce scum, but any scum is easy enough to skim off before bottling the jam. Don't confuse this with jam making sugar which has added pectin. Pectin is needed for setting but it's usually cheaper to buy the sugar and pectin separately.

Lemon juice or citric acid is often added to jams. The acidity helps the setting process and helps cut through the sweetness of the sugar, enhancing the flavour of the fruit.

The substance that actually causes the jam to set is pectin, which reacts with the sugars. Some fruits are naturally high in pectin but others are low and you can buy pectin to add to the jam to ensure a good set.

Pectin is available either as a liquid solution, which has a problem in that once the bottle is opened it will not keep well, or as a powder with indefinite storage life.

General Jam Making Method

Stage 1 – Cook the Fruit

Prepare the fruit; washing and draining well, removing any stalks or stones, etc. Check the weight at this stage and then place into a large saucepan or preserving pan.

Simmer the fruit with any lemon juice or citric acid called for by the recipe to soften it thoroughly and release the pectin. Usually there is enough juice so that you won't need to add any water but sometimes just a little water is required to prevent burning on the base of the pan.

Stage 2 – Test for Pectin

This is the stage that people often miss out and then complain that their jam won't set. You need to establish there is enough pectin in the fruit to enable a good set.

Take one teaspoonful of the cooked fruit juice and put into a glass. Allow this to cool down and then add three teaspoonfuls of methylated spirits.

If a large clot forms in the juice, adequate pectin has been extracted and the sugar may be added to the pan.

If there is a medium amount of pectin, several small clots will form, you may need to cook for longer to extract more pectin or add additional pectin.

If there is very little pectin content, it will break into small pieces and additional pectin will have to be added.

Stage 3 – Adding the Sugar and Boiling Rapidly to Setting Point

You'll find it helpful to warm your sugar before adding it to the fruit. We sterilize our jars in the oven so it's on anyway. Just put the sugar in a heatproof dish with the jars.

Add the warmed sugar and stir away from the heat until the sugar has dissolved. Once the sugar has dissolved, return to the heat and bring to a rapid boil for 5 to 10 minutes, stirring occasionally to prevent the jam sticking to the bottom of the pan and burning.

Remove the pan from the heat and test to see if the jam has reached setting point by one of the following ways:

Put 1 teaspoon of jam onto a cold saucer and allow to cool for a minute. Push the surface gently with your fingertip and, if the surface has a skin that wrinkles, setting point is reached.

Dip a wooden spoon into the jam, remove it, and after a second or two tilt the spoon so that the jam drips. If the jam is almost set and the drops run together in large flakes, setting point has been reached.

Dip a sugar thermometer in hot water, stir the jam, then immerse the thermometer into it. Do not allow the bulb to touch the bottom of the pan as it may break. If the temperature is around 105°C (220°F) setting point has been reached.

Stage 4 – Clarifying and Bottling Up

While you are making your jam, put your washed jars and lids into the oven set at Gas Mark 1 (140°C/275°F) to sterilize them. Never pour hot jam into cold jars, the thermal shock will most likely shatter the glass.

Once you know that your jam has reached setting point, turn off the heat and leave for a couple of minutes. You may find a scum develops on the surface. This can be skimmed off with a spoon or add a knob of butter and stir it in, which will remove it. The scum isn't anything bad; it just looks unsightly.

Place the jars on a heatproof surface and pour the jam into them. A ladle is handy for this along with the jam funnel mentioned above.

Strawberry Jam

Makes about 3 kg (6½ lb) of jam

2 kg (4 lb) strawberries
Juice of 2 lemons
2 kg (4 lb) sugar

1. Hull the strawberries, wash and drain well.
2. Put into a preserving pan with the lemon juice.
3. Simmer gently until the fruit is soft.
4. Test for pectin.
5. Add the sugar, stirring until it has dissolved.
6. Bring to the boil and boil rapidly for 5–10 minutes until the jam sets when tested.
7. Remove the scum and leave to cool slightly so that the fruit will not rise in the jars.
8. Pot and seal while still warm.

Raspberry Jam

Makes around 3 kg (6½ lb) of jam

2 kg (4 lb) raspberries
2 kg (4 lb) sugar

1. Wash the fruit if necessary and drain well.
2. Put into a preserving pan.
3. Simmer until some juice has been extracted.
4. Test for pectin.
5. Add the sugar, stirring until it has dissolved.
6. Bring to the boil and boil rapidly for 5–10 minutes until the jam sets when tested.
7. Remove the scum and leave to cool slightly so that the fruit will not rise in the jars.
8. Pot and seal while still warm.

Do be careful: your jam is still extremely hot and the jars will become so too.

Seal the lids, clean off any spills with methylated spirits and then label with name and date when cooled. Store in a cool dark place.

Problems

It happens to the best of us – we test for pectin, test for setting point and then bottle up only to find that the jam is still runny the next day. Don't despair. Pour the jam back into the pan and re-boil for a minute or two. Carefully check for setting but if it isn't working add some pectin. Don't over-do it though. We've managed to go from one extreme to the other and end up with solid, cut-with-a-knife jam.

Don't forget to re-sterilize the jars before re-potting.

Once you've got to grips with jams, you can expand your repertoire and include conserves, curds and fruit cheeses. We've explained these in detail in our book, *Easy Jams, Chutneys and Preserves*.

Damson Jam

Makes about 3 kg (6½ lb) of jam

As damsons have loads of pectin, this is a very easy jam to make.

2 kg (4 lb) damsons
150 ml (5 fl oz) water
2 kg (4 lb) sugar

1. Wash and wipe the damsons. Pick over to remove stalks.
2. Put into a pan with the water and simmer gently until the fruit is soft, occasionally pressing the damsons against the sides of the pan to break open and release the stones.
3. Remove the stones.
4. Test for pectin.
5. Remove from the heat, add the sugar, stirring until it has dissolved.
6. Return to the hob, bring to the boil and boil rapidly for about 10 minutes until the jam sets when tested.
7. Remove the remainder of the stones as they rise to the surface.
8. Remove the scum and pot and seal whilst still hot. Label when cool.

Blackcurrant Jam

Makes about 4 kg (8 lb) of jam

Traditionally, this recipe calls for a higher proportion of sugar than fruit –
up to 1½ times. We've tried it both ways and found no real advantage to using
extra sugar. The main point when making this jam is to make sure that you
do not cook the fruit too quickly or the skins will toughen.
The skins must be well and truly soft before the sugar is added.

2 kg (4 lb) blackcurrants
1.5 litres (55 fl oz) water
2 kg (4 lb) sugar

1. Remove the stalks from the currants, then wash and drain carefully.
2. Put into the pan with the water, bring to the boil, then simmer until the fruit is soft and pulpy and the contents of the pan are reduced by about a third. Take care not to cook the fruit too quickly or the skins will toughen. You'll need to stir frequently whilst the pulp is reducing to prevent sticking.
3. Test for pectin.
4. Remove from the heat, add the sugar, stirring until the sugar has dissolved.
5. Return to the hob, bring to the boil and boil rapidly until the jam sets when tested.
6. Remove the scum and pot and seal while still hot. Label when cool.

Jellies

The process for making jellies is very similar to that of jams except there is the additional stage after the initial boiling of the fruit – straining the fruit pulp through a jelly bag. This is the only piece of additional equipment that you'll need.

Jelly bags are usually made of nylon or cotton and are fairly easy to obtain.

You'll obviously need some type of drip stand to suspend the bag. These can be purchased or you can improvise with an upside-down kitchen stool as shown here.

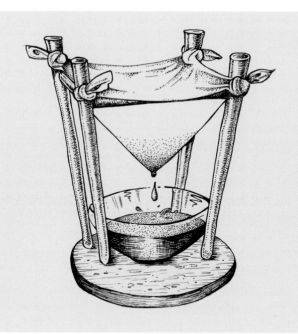

Don't be tempted to squeeze the bag to hasten the dripping process as this tends to make the final jelly cloudy.

It's difficult to give an approximate yield for jellies as it does depend on how much juice you manage to extract.

Redcurrant Jelly

This is a basic currant recipe. You can use blackcurrants or even white currants instead, despite their inferior flavour. Currants are rich in pectin so you should have no problem with setting.

2 kg (4 lb) redcurrants
1.5 litres (55 fl oz) water
500 g (1 lb) sugar per 600 ml (20 fl oz) of juice obtained

1. Wash and drain the redcurrants. Pick over to remove any unsound fruit but do not remove the stalks.
2. Put the fruit into a pan with the water and simmer until the fruit is pulpy.
3. Test for pectin. Turn into a jelly bag and leave to strain for 3–4 hours.
4. Measure the juice and heat in a pan. Add 500 g (1 lb) of warmed sugar to each 600 ml (20 fl oz) of juice, stirring until the sugar has dissolved.
5. Bring to the boil and boil rapidly until the jelly sets when tested.
6. Remove the scum and pot into hot sterilized jars and seal.

Blackberry Jelly

You can replace the cooking apples with crab apples in this recipe as they are both high in pectin – the apples help to make up for the blackberries (especially the late ones) lacking pectin.

500 g (1 lb) cooking apples
2 kg (4 lb) blackberries
750 ml (26 fl oz) water
Juice of 1 lemon
350 g (12 oz) sugar per 600 ml (20 fl oz) of juice obtained

1. Wash and wipe the apples, cut into quarters, but do not remove the skins or cores.
2. Wash and drain the blackberries and pick over to remove any unsound fruit and stalks.
3. Put the apples into a pan with the water and lemon juice and simmer until pulpy.
4. Add the blackberries and continue simmering until the blackberries are soft.
5. Test for pectin.
6. Turn into a jelly bag and leave overnight to strain.
7. Measure the juice and heat in a pan.
8. Add 350 g (12 oz) warmed sugar to each 600 ml (20 fl oz) of juice, stirring until the sugar has dissolved.
9. Bring to the boil and boil rapidly until the jelly sets when tested.
10. Remove the scum and pot into hot sterilized jars and seal. Label when cool.

Marmalades

Marmalade making is very similar to jam making but the rind needs to be cooked for much longer so more water is required. The fruit is simmered until the rind is soft and the volume of liquid has reduced by about half. Jelly marmalades are made in the same way but are strained through a jelly bag after the fruit has been cooked and strips of rind are then added.

Any citrus fruit can be used for making marmalade: bitter or sweet oranges, lemons, grapefruit, tangerines, satsumas and ugli fruit, on their own or in various combinations. Flavourings such as ginger, whisky, rum, brandy, treacle and apricots can be added but the citrus flavour must predominate.

The same equipment is required for making marmalade that is used for jams and jellies with the addition of a good sharp knife and a juice extractor.

Pectin

The pectin in citrus fruit is contained in the white pith and pips. Extra acid is often added to ensure a good set as only about 500 g (1 lb) of fruit is used to make 1.5 kg (3 lb) of marmalade.

Preparation of Fruit

- Wash and lightly scrub the fruit and dry thoroughly.
- Slice or shred the fruit according to preference and tie the pips in a muslin bag. If you dislike pith in your marmalade, remove it from the peel, chop thoroughly and add this in with the pips to the muslin bag.

General Method for Making Thick Marmalade

- Put all of the ingredients into a pan, except for the sugar, with the pips tied inside a muslin bag. Bring to the boil and simmer gently until the peel is soft and the contents of the pan have been reduced to half its original bulk. This will take 1½–2 hours.
- Lift out the bag of pips, squeezing it against the side of the pan with a wooden spoon.

- Test for pectin the same way as for jams. If the clot is poor or thready, add the juice of two lemons to each 1 kg (2 lb) fruit used and continue simmering the fruit until a good pectin clot is obtained.
- Remove from the heat and stir in the sugar until it has dissolved.
- Return to the hob, bring to the boil and boil rapidly for 15–35 minutes until the marmalade sets when tested.
- Test for setting just like jam – put a little marmalade onto a cold plate, cool, and if the marmalade wrinkles when touched with the finger it is cooked sufficiently and will set. Always draw the pan away from the heat when testing for "set", otherwise the marmalade may over cook.
- Add a knob of butter or a few drops of glycerine and stir in to reduce the amount of scum and then skim off using a perforated spoon. Do this as soon as possible after setting point has been reached as, if left much longer, the scum tends to cling to the pieces of peel.
- Leave the marmalade to cool slightly so that the peel will not rise to the top of the jar.
- Pour the marmalade into clean, dry, hot sterilized jars and seal.

Old English Marmalade

Makes about 3 kg (6½ lb) of marmalade

Seville (sour) oranges are large, seedy fruits that are rich in pectin.
In England this marmalade is traditionally made during the short season after
Christmas when these bitter oranges are available in the shops.
In the southern states there are many varieties of this type of orange
that can be grown.

1 kg (2 lb) Seville oranges
2 lemons
2.4 litres (80 fl oz) water
2 kg (4 lb) sugar – of which at least 500 g (1 lb) should be brown sugar

1. Wash and dry the fruit. Cut in half and squeeze out the juice. Remove the pips, inside skin and pith. Tie these in a piece of muslin.
2. Cut the peel and fruit chunkily.
3. Put into a pan with the muslin bag and the water. Bring to the boil and simmer gently until the peel is really soft and the volume has reduced to about half of its original bulk. This will take between 1½–2 hours.
4. Lift out the muslin bag, squeezing it against the side of the pan with a wooden spoon.
5. Test for pectin (not normally a problem).
6. Remove from the heat and stir in warmed sugar until it has dissolved.
7. Return to the hob, bring to the boil and boil rapidly for 15–35 minutes until the marmalade sets when tested.
8. Allow to cool slightly, stir, and then pot and seal whilst still hot.

Lemon or Lime Marmalade

Makes about 3 kg (6½ lb) of marmalade

You can make this marmalade with either lemons or limes
or a mixture of both, which works well.

1 kg (2 lb) lemons or limes
2.4 litres (80 fl oz) water
2 kg (4 lb) sugar

1. Wash and dry the fruit. Cut in half and squeeze out the juice. Remove the pips and tie these in a piece of muslin.
2. Slice or shred the fruit.
3. Put into a pan along with the juice, water and the bag of pips. Bring to the boil and simmer gently until the peel is really soft. This will take between 1½–2 hours.
4. Lift out the bag of pips, squeezing it against the side of the pan with a wooden spoon.
5. Test for pectin. This is rarely lacking.
6. Remove from the heat and stir in the sugar until it has dissolved.
7. Return to the hob, bring to the boil and boil rapidly for 15–35 minutes until the marmalade sets when tested.
8. Remove any scum and leave to cool slightly.
9. Stir, pot and seal whilst still hot.

12

Juicing, Cider and Perry

●

N ow we know it's fashionable to enjoy fresh juices of all sorts of fruits and vegetables and you can buy some pretty expensive machines to do it for you, but that's not the subject of this chapter. We're talking about coping with gluts of fruit, basically apples and pears, by turning them into juice and storing it.

Most berries can also be juiced, but with many of them you may prefer to convert them into a country wine, which is a subject to itself and a little outside of the scope of this book.

If you find yourself with a big old apple or pear tree, then you're likely to have so much fruit you just can't eat it in a year, but it's a tragedy to waste it. The first thing is how to extract the juice but before that a word of warning. You can use windfalls for juice but do watch out for wasps when collecting them. It's amazing how the nasty things are hidden under the fruit you are picking up. Even gloves don't offer 100 per cent protection as the wasps just target your wrist. Or perhaps that's just our bad luck.

Tradition has it that rough cider was made with apples regardless of their condition but we prefer to cut off any badly bruised or rotting sections and then quarter the fruit before crushing.

You can crush the fruit in a tough plastic bucket using the end of a piece of wood but beyond one bucket this will get very tiring. Automating a little, there is a device you can buy called a Pulpmaster which attaches to an electric drill. It is just a blade that cuts the apples up and you can buy it with a bin. The shaft goes through the bin lid which stops the contents splashing everywhere, or you can construct your own using an old fermenting bin and drilling the hole for the shaft through it so you just buy the blade attachment.

For serious quantities of fruit you really need a purpose-made crusher. This pulls the fruit in and crushes it to a pulp. They can be bought cheaply but we'd advise buying the best you can afford. The better ones will last a lifetime and you can often pick up a quality fruit crusher and press secondhand off internet auction sites for less than a cheap new one.

Once you have your crushed fruit, it's time to press the juice out. The most efficient and easiest method is to use a press. We have a combined crusher and press which makes things very simple. The crushed apples go into a filter bag inside the press and then it's a matter of removing the crushing head and putting the screw down press on.

Alternatively, you can try putting the crushed apples into filter bags and applying pressure by hand. A proper press will get far more juice out of your fruit for you though.

Once you have pressed your fruit, you are left with the pulp. You can consider it a waste product – it composts quite well – or use it mixed with oats, etc., as the basis of homemade granola bars.

Often when you press your own juice you will find it quite dark and murky compared with commercial juices. Now it can be argued that your homemade juice is better for you as the murkiness is caused by small particles of fruit that have gone through the filter bag. However, that's not much use if the children take one look and decide you're trying to poison them!

To clarify the juice you can drip-filter through a small mesh jelly bag or even coffee filter papers but this will take a long time and can be a bit disruptive in the smaller kitchen. Another method is to put the juice into a tall jug or covered (food grade) bucket and add a teaspoon of pectolase, aka pectolyase. This is an enzyme used to degrade pectin when making wines and is cheaply available from

wine making suppliers. Leave overnight in a cool place or preferably in the refrigerator if you have the space. The effect will be to cause the particles to clump together and sink to the bottom. You then carefully pour off the clarified juice.

Your juice will keep for a while in the fridge or can be frozen in containers. We have used the waxed cardboard containers that shop-bought juice often comes in for this.

Freshly made juice may well be too tart for the family's taste. The simple answer to this is to taste and add a little sugar if need be. Personally we prefer simple sugar to complex chemical sweeteners, but you could use those if you prefer.

Your juice will contain a number of microbes and yeasts which are floating in the air or on the skin of the fruit. They'll do you no harm in fresh juice but if you just leave your juice on the side they'll start trying to convert the sugars to alcohol. To store fruit juice outside of the freezer you need to bottle it, killing the yeasts in the process. See Chapter 7, Bottling (Canning).

Cider and Perry

The traditional way of making cider or perry, which is just cider made with pears, was pretty hit and miss. The juice went into a barrel and the natural yeasts would ferment it to cider. Some brews were good, some not so. Of course, those old-time farmers had their own methods and secret additives. We're pretty sure the dead rat to add flavour was just an urban myth…

The quality of the cider was actually quite important to the farmer in pre-mechanization days. They depended on seasonal itinerant workers to get the harvest in and the farms with a reputation for good cider could attract the better workers. Good strains of yeast would linger in the barrel so these were re-used from year to year.

Nowadays we can easily obtain a consistently good cider by applying a little science and buying in good strains rather than relying on wild yeasts to do the work.

You'll need a little equipment, but this can be used from year to year so consider it an investment.

A larger fermenting vessel with airlock, as sold for home beer making, is ideal. Don't forget to sterilize it before you start. We want to make sure that the wild yeasts are not around.

Measure the specific gravity of your juice. You use a tool called a hydrometer for this. For the best result it should be 1070 or over. If

it's lower, you need to add some sugar syrup to feed the yeasts, taking the specific gravity up to 1070. If the specific gravity is above 1070, don't worry – you're going to have strong sweet cider.

A rough guide to how much sugar to add is 5 oz per UK gallon, 6 oz per US gallon, 150 g per 5 litres, to raise the specific gravity by 10. Dissolve the sugar in hot water. It's not critical though. One of the joys in homemade produce is the variation between batches. Shop-bought products are always boringly consistent – usually good but never great or special.

You can use clarified or murky juice as you wish. Many of the solids will precipitate out during fermentation anyway. However, if the fermentation is vigorous, the particles in murky juice may be pushed up and block the airlock.

The expert home cider makers will often mix different juices, perhaps some sweet dessert apples for the sugar content and some crab apple juice to add bite to the final product. This is a skill that takes time to develop so, initially, just work with what you have.

Those experts also aim to control the pH of the cider, adding chalk to increase it, or malic acid to reduce it, to an ideal 3.9 or 4.0, but to be honest we've never found it worthwhile going to those lengths.

Once the juice is in the fermenting vessel, add a finely crushed Campden tablet dissolved in warm water per gallon (5 litres) and leave for 24 to 48 hours. Campden tablets are sodium metabisulphite and release sulphur dioxide which kills off the wild yeasts.

Now add a commercial champagne yeast, available very cheaply from home winemaking suppliers. If you have difficulty finding a champagne yeast, which is unlikely, any general wine yeast will suffice. You don't need to add any yeast nutrient as a rule, but it can do no harm.

Place the fermenting vessel somewhere warm – room temperature is fine. Initially there will be a rush with bubbles of gas popping through the airlock constantly but this will slow down after a couple of weeks as fermentation comes to an end.

When the cider has finished fermenting, check the specific gravity which should now be around 1005. Rack it off to get rid of the sediments and leave for a couple of days to settle further. If need be, rack it off again using finings (available from home winemaking suppliers) if it won't clear and you are bothered about the appearance.

"Racking off" is the term for transferring wine or cider from one vessel to another, leaving the sediment at the bottom behind. It's undertaken by siphoning. Just use a thin plastic tube, one end in the vessel above the sediment and the other in the new vessel which should be lower than the full vessel. Suck on one end to pull the liquid through and start the flow.

Now you can add one Campden tablet per gallon to stop fermentation by killing the yeast before bottling. You can use plastic fizzy drink bottles for cider or glass if you prefer. Cider has a nasty habit of restarting fermentation, so be careful with glass bottles as they can explode. Loosen the tops occasionally to release any pressure build ups. Alternatively, keep in the fermenting vessel and have a party.

Don't forget that you can also make perry – pear cider – in exactly the same way. However, do use some yeast nutrient with perry; it seems to need it.

13
Drying

●

D
rying, as a method of food preservation, probably pre-dates civilization. In hot climates it is so easy: just leave whatever you wish to dry on a stone in the sun. Even today, Punjab fishermen dry their catches by simply hanging the fish on lines in the sun and wind.

Drying works by simply dehydrating the food. Removing the moisture from the food prevents the growth of bacteria and moulds. Although properly dried food is safe from microbial action, there's still the risk of insect and even rodent damage. Storing in air-tight jars or tins will generally prevent this. Keeping your dried foods at a temperature below 21°C (70°F) will also help with insect damage as many of the tiny insects that like to dine on our foods prefer it warm.

Light, especially direct sunlight, can bleach dried foods, especially herbs, so store in dark glass jars or keep in a dark cupboard or store room.

Drying Methods

There are three things we need to provide to dehydrate anything.

- **Dry air** – as far as possible. Drying in a humid atmosphere will not work. Moulds will develop and we replace the moisture being lost by the food as fast as we take it out.
- **Warmth** – but not cooking heat. We want to encourage drying but not so hot as to start a cooking process.

- **Draught or Airflow**. Passing air over the drying food takes away the moisture and replaces with dry air ready to absorb yet more moisture.

Whatever equipment or method we use, those are the conditions we are trying to achieve.

Air Drying

This is simple, needing no equipment, and just involves hanging the food to be dried in somewhere warm with a decent amount of airflow. We have covered this in detail in Chapter 18, Herbs. We also dry our chilli peppers in this way.

Commercial Drying Machine

There's a wide range of machines on the market with varying capacities and features. They used to be quite expensive but in recent years low-cost models have appeared on the market. Our cheap dryer has multiple trays and is very compact but the only control is an on-

off switch. More sophisticated models have temperature controls and timers, but they cost more to buy, of course.

In our experience, the less sophisticated the equipment is, the more reliable it will be in the long run. Using such equipment just involves you having to remember to switch off when you've finished and to vary positions to partially control the heat on the food.

We bought our machine to replace our homemade drying cabinet which was effective but took up more room in storage and didn't survive being dropped when we brought it down from the attic!

Homemade Drying Cabinet

You can build a simple drying cabinet for next to nothing at home if you have a little skill.

Build a box from wood (thin plywood or whatever you have to hand) or even use a stout cardboard box and completely seal it except for a few holes in the sides towards the bottom under the heat source and at the top to allow ventilation. Obviously, some sort of "door" needs to be allowed for placing whatever you are drying inside.

A heat source is also needed and electricity is most convenient and safe. We found that the heat from a 60 watt light bulb gave the right temperature for a box of about 2½ feet by 1½ feet (75 x 45 cm). The bulb needs to go in the bottom, protected from any dripping juices by a perforated piece of wood or cardboard suspended above it. Better still, use a thin metal sheet with holes drilled through. This spreads and evens the heat rising above.

Ventilation is important so that the warm air can circulate freely throughout the whole cabinet, so the food should be placed on either perforated trays, trays or racks with wooden slats and a cheesecloth or muslin base. Wire cake trays or weldmesh cut to size with cheesecloth or muslin stretched over them and fastened at the corners with pins can also be used. The fabric allows air through but stops the imprint of the wire from marking the fruit or vegetable.

If new cheesecloth or muslin is used, wash and dry before use or it could give the food an unpleasant flavour.

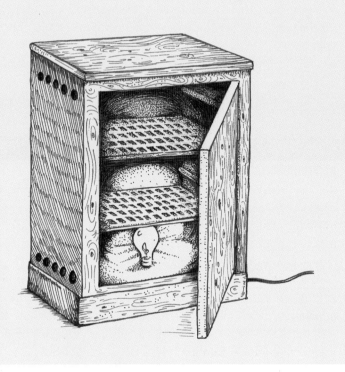

Unlike the commercial bought dryers with their thermostats and timers, you need to use your judgement as to when things are ready.

Solar Dryer

Many years ago we built a solar dryer. Effectively it was a box lined with aluminium foil with ventilation holes at the base at the rear and through the top at the front with wire shelves and a glass front. The concept was that the sun heated the chamber, drawing in cold air at the base, passing it through the cabinet and out through the top.

In the blazing hot summer of 1976 it managed to cook anything placed in it for more than a few minutes, which was not the desired result. Since then we've been waiting for another good summer.

Solar dryers do make a lot of sense if you live in the right climate and can adjust them to achieve the temperature you want. Sadly not for the UK.

Oven Drying

You can use an ordinary oven to dry foods but the oven needs to be capable of working at a very low temperature: 50°C (122°F). Electric fan ovens that will work this low are great, followed by solid fuel ranges with cool ovens and finally gas. Gas tends to be more humid so not so good.

With a solid-fuel, wood or oil-fired oven like an Aga or Rayburn, the heat remaining after cooking sessions can be utilized. This may mean that the drying process is not continuous and has to be carried out over several days but this should not affect the quality of the finished product. Use the simmering oven in solid-fuel cookers for drying and do allow for adequate ventilation.

You can leave the door open to keep the temperature down and airflow up but please be careful. Young children have a way of getting into trouble in the blink of the eye. Cats and dogs know that ovens are where the delicious smells come from, so leaving the door open is an invitation to climb in.

When drying either fruit or vegetables in the oven, check the temperature occasionally during the drying process. It can be very hard to check such low temperatures, even with an oven thermometer, but a guide to the right temperature is to put your hand in the oven un-gloved – you should be able to keep it there in comfort for at least 30 seconds.

Microwave Drying

You can use a microwave for drying herbs successfully but we've not tried drying other foods in there and doubt it would work for them.

What to dry

The most popular food for drying would have to be herbs. There are few kitchens where you won't find at least a couple of jars of dried herbs. We have covered drying herbs in some depth in Chapter 18, Herbs.

Fruits can be dried and are quite palatable, in some cases delicious, in their dried form. Dried fruits have always been a popular line in the health food shops and there is no reason why you can't make your own.

Vegetables can be dried but as a general rule they're not worth the bother. For example, root crops can be much better stored in peat or sand boxes in almost fresh conditions. Just because you can dry something doesn't mean you should dry it. Sweetcorn can be dried, but is really far, far better frozen and even bottled. The only time we would dry it is if we had a large amount and wanted it for the hens.

The real exceptions to the general rule on drying vegetables are tomatoes and beans. However, when we had a problem with white rot causing our stored onions to rot we did dry some as a way of saving some of the crop as we're fanatical about avoiding "store-bought" vegetables and being self-sufficient. It was a lot of fuss for a low-cost vegetable.

Drying Onions

Use medium to large onions. Peel and cut them into ¼ inch (5 mm) slices.

Separate the slices into rings – the very small centres are difficult to dry satisfactorily so it's best to use them up for cooking fresh.

Dip the onion rings into boiling water for about 30 seconds, drain and pat dry with a towel or kitchen roll paper.

Spread the onion rings onto trays and dry at a temperature not higher than Gas Mark 0/65°C/150°F until they are crisp and dry. (This will take about 3–4 hours.)

Once cooled, pack into botles or jars with airtight lids. Store in a dry, dark place.

When required, soak them in warm water for about 30 minutes. If they are to be fried or grilled, pat them dry with kitchen roll paper before use.

Dried Tomatoes

We have all seen sun-dried tomatoes, often in jars of oil, but they are more a processed product than dried to store. We have covered dried tomatoes in Chapter 14, Storing in Oil. Our own feeling is that when dealing with a glut, freezing or bottling are more practical but dried tomatoes do go well in small quantities in a salad and some pasta dishes.

Dried Beans and Peas

It's perfectly possible to dry runner or French beans but they would be better, salted, bottled or frozen. However, haricot beans, where we eat the bean rather than the pod, and marrowfat peas are good subjects for drying.

We have covered the traditional air-drying method for haricot beans or the beans that form in runners if left too long on the plant in Chapter 16, Vegetables. Incidentally, that's the same method you use if you want to save your own seed for next year's planting.

The natural drying method isn't the most reliable in the British summer though and is not the most effective for peas. Don't dry young sweet peas or petits pois. They are much better frozen. Save your drying for large mature marrowfat peas that will be ending up in soups, stews and mushy peas (check out the recipe for mushy peas in Chapter 16, Vegetables; it really is delicious).

Pod your peas or beans and drop into cold water. The reason for this is that you may well have a few pea maggots and they will float out in the water. Now blanch for about three minutes. Since they inevitably slip through the holes in a blanching basket, we just drop them straight into the blanching water and then use a flour sieve to fish them out.

Don't cool after blanching. Just dry them on a towel before spreading onto trays and drying. Ideally dry at a temperature starting at Gas Mark 0/50°C/120°F and then increase the temperature slowly up to Gas Mark 0/65°C/150°F.

The beans and peas are dry when they are quite crisp. Depending on their size, this takes between 2–3 hours. Pack in tightly corked bottles or airtight containers and store in a dry, dark place.

The only real drawback with dried beans is that they require soaking prior to use. If you are the sort of person who plans ahead with your meals, then it's no problem but if you are the type of person who gets home and then decides what to eat, dried beans can be difficult.

Usually you should soak dried beans and peas in cold water for about 12 hours to re-hydrate them fully before use. If you're in a hurry there is a way round which we came across in Rose Elliott's excellent *The Bean Book*. Simply put your beans or peas into a large saucepan with plenty of cold water. Bring to the boil and boil vigorously for two or three minutes. Remove from the heat, cover the pan and leave for three quarters to an hour by which time they should be re-hydrated.

Drying Plums, Apricots, Nectarines and Peaches

Plums and apricots can be dried whole but, if they are on the large size, they are better halved and stoned. Peaches and nectarines need to be halved and stoned.

Wash the fruit, pat dry with kitchen roll and place the fruit in a single layer on the drying tray.

If they are halved, they should be placed with the cut side upwards so that the juice does not run out.

Start the drying process at Gas Mark 0/50°C/120°F. The skins will burst and some of the juice will be lost if they are dried at a higher temperature.

Once the skins begin to shrivel, the temperature can be raised to Gas Mark 0/65°C/150°F to complete the drying process.

When finished, remove the trays from the heat source and leave to cool at room temperature for 12 hours. Pack the fruit in wooden or cardboard boxes lined with greaseproof paper or, better, airtight jars or containers and store in a very dry place.

Drying Apples and Pears

Peel and core the apples or pears.

Apples should be cut into ¼ inch (5 mm) rings and pears into halves or quarters depending on their size.

Place the pieces into a bowl of cold salted water immediately for a few minutes to prevent discoloration. Use about 2 oz (56 g) of salt to each UK gallon (4.5 litres) of water.

Lift out with a perforated spoon and pat fully dry with kitchen paper roll.

Place the pieces of fruit in single layers on the drying tray and cover with a piece of muslin to keep the fruit clean whilst it is drying. You might like to try sprinkling a little ground cinnamon or cloves on the fruit before drying to add a special flavour.

Dry at Gas Mark 0/65°C/150°F to Gas Mark ½/90°C/200°F for around 4 to 6 hours. Check that they are fully dry by pressing two or three pieces together and, if they feel rubbery and spring back into shape, they are ready.

Remove from the heat source and leave for about 12 hours. If flies are about, cover with muslin or cheesecloth.

Pack into wooden or cardboard boxes lined with greaseproof paper or, better, airtight jars or containers and store in a very dry place.

Grapes to Raisins

Raisins are simply dried grapes. In the Mediterranean, people simply take the bunches of seedless grapes and lay them in the sun for a couple of weeks before removing them from the stems and spreading on trays to dry further.

Grapes really need a long period of relatively gentle warmth, say 30°C (86°F) to dry. Such conditions are not so easy to achieve in colder and less sunny northern climes where grapes are better turned into wine.

Berries

Most berries can be dried. With larger berries, like strawberries, they are best sliced before drying. Berries can take a surprisingly long time to dry and we prefer to store them in other ways.

Fruit Leather

Most fruits can be made into fruit leather. The method is quite simple. First make a thick purée from the fruit. Avoid adding any water if you can. The purée should be as dry as you can get it.

Spread thinly, 5 mm or ¼ inch thick, onto a tray and dry in your preferred method, oven or dryer. In an oven use a very low temperature, Gas Mark 0/60°C/140°F for about 8 to 12 hours. The leather is best stored in airtight containers in the refrigerator and can be used cut up into chips in cakes, ice cream or desserts.

14
Storing in Oil

●

S toring in oil is a traditional method that probably dates back to the beginnings of civilization when man discovered olive oil in the fertile crescent of the Mediterranean. Nowadays it is used more often as a way of producing flavoured oil than an actual storage method and the main vegetables used are garlic, chilli peppers and dried tomatoes. Not only can you use the produce, the flavoured oil can be used for salad dressing or in cooking.

The theory is quite simple. The produce is covered in the oil, which excludes air so preventing the growth of spoiling organisms.

For years we stored in oil by simply placing the produce in a sterilized jar and filling the jar with oil, agitating to get any air bubbles out before sealing the jar. However, when we published this on our website we were deluged with emails warning that we could get botulism from this and would likely die in short order.

Having researched this terrible risk we discovered that it was first mentioned on a Canadian website in reference to an outbreak of botulism from a restaurant in Vancouver. This was picked up and repeated on other websites, growing in threat and risk until it became a fact as far as casual searchers were concerned that the cold oil storing of peppers or garlic or anything else for that matter was a certain way to kill the poor souls who ate the produce.

We did take this risk seriously and decided to consult a food scientist directly. He explained that there was a theoretical risk that small droplets of water adhering to the vegetable would provide a growing medium for the botulism bacterium and could, therefore, poison consumers.

He couldn't quantify the risk, not being a statistician, but comparisons with being struck by a meteor or winning the big prize on the lottery twice were mentioned. It's a sad sign of our fear of litigation that he wouldn't go on record as saying it was safe although he said he would have no concerns personally about using the method. In fairness, no scientist will ever talk in absolutes since even a miniscule risk is still a risk.

Having tired of explaining and arguing this endlessly, we now only recommend the hot oil storage method.

Use an oil that doesn't have a strong flavour; it will be overwhelmed by the garlic or chilli flavour anyway. A good quality olive oil is fine, or even just sunflower oil. You don't need to pay the premium for extra virgin oil.

Prepare the contents: de-seeding, washing and thoroughly drying peppers before slicing into strips or removing the paper from garlic cloves, slicing the larger cloves lengthways in half.

Sterilize washed clean jars and lids by heating in a low oven for ten minutes or more. This will drive out any moisture and heat the jars so they do not shatter under thermal shock when you add the hot oil. Ensure the contents are dry, then place them in the jar, and pour on oil that has been heated to 140°C (285°F) or higher. This has the same effect as the commercial canning botulinum cook of 121°C (250°F) for three minutes.

Seal the jar, ensuring it is airtight. Keep in a dark cupboard for up to four months, after this it begins to lose flavour. After opening, the jar should be kept in a fridge and the contents used within two weeks.

The hot oil will, of course, affect the flavour but you are perfectly safe unless that meteor plunges through your roof.

Here are a few recipes for storing in oil, using the safe hot oil method although the original recipes used cold oil.

Globe Artichoke Hearts in Oil

Wash the artichokes and simmer in a large saucepan of well salted water until tender, usually about 20 minutes. Remove the outer leaves, thistles, etc. to just leave the hearts.

Place in pre-heated jars with some bay leaves, cracked black peppercorns and coriander seeds and pour on heated oil.

Seal the jars and leave for a month for the flavours to infuse before using. They should keep indefinitely. They make a great appetizer for a summer meal or as a centre for a salad.

Aubergine (Eggplant) in Oil

Slice the aubergine into rounds, place into a dish and sprinkle quite thickly with salt to draw out the bitterness. Cover the dish and leave overnight. The next morning rinse off the salt and pat dry with a clean tea towel.

Place a layer of aubergines into pre-heated jars and pour on some hot oil, then add another layer and more oil, pressing down with a spoon to compress the aubergine as you fill the jar.

To flavour, you can add some garlic cloves, bay leaves and sprigs of thyme with a little black pepper as you fill the jar. Leave for a month for the flavours to infuse before using.

Dried Tomatoes in Oil

Easy to make, these tomatoes provide a great addition to many recipes as well as being nice with a salad.

Take firm tomatoes and slice in half. Place on a baking tray cut side up and sprinkle with a little salt or garlic salt. Place a drop or two of oil on each tomato and bake on the lowest heat your oven has until dried out and wrinkled.

Pack into heated jars and cover with hot oil. They will keep well for a year. Just remove with a slotted spoon from the jar as needed, keeping the jar sealed in between.

15
Freezing

●

Freezing food has to be the oldest method known to mankind to preserve food. In fact there is archaeological evidence that Neanderthal man dug pits in the ice and kept his mammoth meat in them!

Moving on six thousand years or so, the great houses of the aristocracy always had an ice house that was filled with winter ice cut from the lake in the grounds. By the mid 1800s ships sailed to the south from the Arctic Circle with cargoes of ice which was cut up and sold in blocks for domestic ice boxes, the pre-cursor of the electric refrigerators that didn't become common until the 1930s. Even then they were very much a luxury item beyond the means of the working classes.

Around this time, Clarence Birdseye (as in Birdseye Fish Fingers) invented a flash freezing process that made commercial frozen foods possible, although it wasn't until after the Second World War that refrigerated distribution systems started to enable frozen foods to be available in the shops in the USA. We in the UK lagged a little behind, of course.

Although a frozen food compartment was built into fridges, it was only in the 1970s that domestic freezers became commonplace and nowadays they are very affordable, especially when purchased second hand.

What Freezer to Buy

If you are seriously growing your own, a large freezer is indispensable for coping with the inevitable gluts and storing the harvest for out of season. We would suggest that a chest freezer is the best buy. Not only are they generally cheaper to buy for a given amount of storage capacity, but they tend to be more economical to run.

The advantages of a chest freezer are:

- They're simple – the more "bells and whistles" the more there is to go wrong.
- You get more into a chest freezer because upright freezers always have wasted space in their drawers.
- Chest freezers are efficient in that if you open the lid the cold air stays in the box rather than flowing out.
- Chest freezers are generally cheaper to buy than equivalent upright models.
- You can get chest freezers in large sizes, great for home food producers. The larger models offer better capacity for your money.

The disadvantages of a chest freezer are:

- They can be difficult to fit into kitchens neatly as the lid is on the top, so you can't fit them under a counter top.
- Things can be buried at the bottom and forgotten. We found the answer for our chest freezer was some large plastic boxes designed for toys, although robust cardboard boxes might do the job.
- Generally they need to be defrosted manually, but that's only a thirty-minute job every six months or so.
- Upright freezers can be more convenient to fit into the kitchen and the drawers are certainly easier to keep in order and find things.

Whichever type you get, make sure you have enough room and a suitable place to keep it. Surprisingly, some freezers will not work properly if the temperature of the room is too low. You need to check that if you are keeping your freezer in an unheated garage shed or cellar. Some upright freezers demand an air gap at the back of the unit. One we looked at needed an air circulation space to the rear of 45 cm which would have almost placed it in the centre of the kitchen!

Check that the freezer is actually capable of freezing food and how much, as well as just keeping it frozen. Surprisingly there are some freezers on the market that are incapable of fast freezing any reasonable quantity of food.

When buying a freezer, check the energy rating. All stores (including online stores) in the UK should clearly display the energy rating. Choose one "A+" or "A" rated. Outside the UK check the efficiency with the supplier. Efficient freezers using less energy are better for the environment and your pocket.

Although the basic idea of an A rated (Energy Star) freezer is better than B rated (Energy Saving) and so forth, we found a surprising anomaly. We found that a C rated chest freezer used about the same amount of electricity as an A+ rated upright of slightly lower capacity. This may have been because the modern upright incorporated an automatic defrost system. These seem to add considerably to the running costs.

One device we are grateful to have is a Savaplug. At the time of writing, these are no longer available since the manufacturers are bringing out a new model but you may find one on Ebay or similar.

We tested our Savaplug on a number of freezers ranging from a very old upright to a modern A+ rated chest freezer. We paid about £20 each for the plugs and using an electricity monitor calculated savings ranging from £10 a year on the modern freezer to £46 a year on the old upright. Those savings were based on an electricity cost of 11.7p/KWh. We also checked with an electronic maximum/minimum thermometer and there was no degradation in the freezer performance; they all held stable temperatures as set below -18°C (0°F).

Refrigeration and the Environment

There has been quite a lot of talk in the green movements about refrigeration of food, especially as the increase in living standards in India, China and other developing countries means there will be millions more fridges and freezers on the planet in years to come.

There's no argument that refrigeration uses energy, both in the manufacture of the equipment and running it. However, modern equipment no longer uses refrigerant gases that contribute to ozone depletion and increasing global warming.

We admit to not having the skills to fully cost the environmental impact of home freezing foodstuffs but it does seem self-evident that any impact is more than compensated for by the savings made from home growing. The "food miles" acquired by a package of seeds in the mail is negligible in comparison to the miles accumulated by a commercial package of frozen peas grown in this country, never mind frozen shrimp shipped in from half-way around the globe.

Safety of Freezing

Freezing, correctly done, will keep food safe and nutritious indefinitely. However, the taste and texture of some foods will deteriorate over time, even when frozen. The reason is that freezing down to -18°C (0°F) or lower will stop any bacteria from reproducing. Note that it must be kept at -18°C (0°F) or below continuously. The microbes stay dormant in exactly the same state as they were when frozen, but don't forget that when you defrost and increase temperature, they will come back to life and start to multiply again. Treat your defrosted food as fresh. In fact, because of the freezing process damaging the cells, the lifespan when it is defrosted is reduced.

This is why you should not re-freeze defrosted foods, although you can incorporate once frozen ingredients into a meal, cook that and then freeze that meal safely.

Although microbes are stopped by freezing, enzymes are not stopped, they are just slowed down by the cold. Although this will not make the frozen food unsafe, it can cause the flavour to deteriorate. However, blanching your food before freezing will destroy the enzymes and avoid that problem.

While frozen food will remain safe to eat indefinitely, it makes sense to use the oldest first, so labelling is important. Not to mention that it may be obvious when you freeze which bag is runner beans and which is green peppers but six months later with a bit of ice in the bag, a mistake is easy to make.

Often freezer manufacturers will give some guidance as to how long various foods will keep, which will err on the side of caution. As we've said, foods will keep safely for an indefinite time but the flavour may well deteriorate over time due to those enzymes. We've not noticed any deterioration with properly blanched vegetables after two years.

Fresh Crops for Flavour

It may seem obvious, but the fresher the food you freeze, the better the flavour will be when you come to defrost and eat it. With some vegetable crops, most notably peas and sweetcorn, the sugars will start to turn to starch the moment they are harvested. It's best to plan ahead rather than harvest everything in one go and freeze the next day; instead harvest smaller amounts and freeze on the same day. If you really can't freeze on the same day, putting the crop into the fridge will slow down the conversion process of sugar into starch.

Blanching

We have had countless discussions with people who consider blanching to be unnecessary but the fact is that for long-term storage it is needed. Although vegetables frozen without blanching will be safe indefinitely, the flavour will decline over time due to the enzymes in them. Freezing merely slows, not stops, enzymes from causing deterioration. The blanch destroys the enzymes and so we have enjoyed frozen vegetables that have been stored for nearly three years. Blanching also helps retain vitamin C.

Before you start blanching, get everything in order. Switch the freezer onto "super freeze" so it will be as cold as possible. Usually, the setting just over rides the thermostat, taking the temperature down below the normal -18°C (0°F). Check there is enough room in the freezer and rearrange the contents if needed. Some freezers have a special tray or section that is recommended for freezing down and you want to make sure this is ready.

Next have a check in the ordinary refrigerator. We're going to be using this to pre-chill before freezing so clearing a shelf makes life easy. If you can, adjust the thermostat in the fridge to lower the temperature in there as well.

You're going to need quite a lot of ice, so empty the ice cube trays into a bag (in the freezer) and set more on for freezing.

Make sure the kitchen is cleared for action. You will be using a large pot of boiling water and frequently emptying bowls of cooling water. The last thing you want to be doing when emptying large pots of water is moving things out of the way or tripping over toys on the floor.

For the blanching vessel you want as large a pan as you have, preferably with a lid. We used to use a preserving pan but found a large lidded pan came back to the boil faster and used less energy to maintain a fast boil.

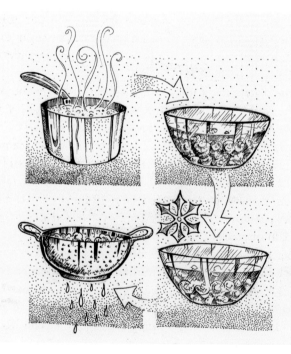

You will also need a blanching basket. This is just a metal wire basket, rather like an old-fashioned chip fryer basket or large sieve, that enables you to easily add and remove your produce from the boiling water.

Next set up another two large pans (the preserving pan now gets used for this), which will hold the cooling water. The first pan is used to take the initial heat off and the second to chill down. Just before you actually start blanching, fill both with cold water and into the second add some ice cubes to really cool the water down. If you have different sized pans, then use the larger as the second chilling pan because you are going to be changing the water in the first pan frequently.

The only other equipment you will need for the blanching is a colander or two. A sieve with a handle is also useful for transferring the blanched vegetables between the two cooling pans.

Fill the blanching pan with water and put on the stove to boil. Whilst waiting for the water to come to the boil, start preparing your produce for blanching. With peas, for example, the sugar to starch process will be speeded up by removing from the pod so we want to minimize the time they wait to blanch.

When the water is at a rolling boil, add a portion of the produce into the blanching basket and place into the water. Ideally you want the water to come back to a fast boil in a minute or less. This will depend on the volume of water and the power of the ring under the pan, so adjust the quantity to try to achieve this. As we said above, placing a lid over will help hold the heat and speed up the process of getting back to a boil. If it takes too long to come back to the boil, use a smaller portion next time. We found we needed about 6 pints of water per 1 lb of produce, about 4 litres to 500 g.

After blanching for the recommended time, which varies according to the type of produce, remove from the blanching water and tip into the first pan of cooling water. Usually you count the blanching time from the time the water starts to boil vigorously again. A timer is invaluable for blanching as the timing is fairly important. You don't want to over-cook things.

Whilst the produce is cooling in the first pan, set the second lot to blanching and then transfer the partially cooled produce from the first pan to the second with its iced water. You will find that your sieve comes in useful for transferring between pans.

You'll probably notice that the water in the first pan is noticeably warmed and will need to change it at this point for fresh cold tap water.

Usually by the time the next batch is ready for the second pan, the produce in there has cooled down and can go into the colander to drain off. Once drained, transfer to the fridge to keep cool until you're ready to bag up for the freezer.

Blanching is one of those tasks that is more complicated to explain than to actually do but hopefully the illustration on page 116 will show how simple it is. After a couple of seasons, you will have turned the whole process into quite an art form!

Just remember that to blanch successfully we need to bring the food up to boiling as fast as possible and, once blanched, reduce the temperature, thereby stopping the cooking process as quickly as we can.

Freezing

Clarence Birdseye discovered that the quality of frozen food was vastly improved by flash freezing. Modern freezing plants utilize liquid nitrogen to freeze foods down in seconds.

The reason is that when you freeze food slowly, it allows large ice crystals to develop and as these expand they burst cells and destroy the texture of the food. In other words, slow freezing produces mushy food. Fast freezing produces much smaller ice crystals and the final texture of the defrosted produce will be much improved.

Because of this, it's important not to overload your freezer. If you put too much in at the same time it will take much longer to freeze down and can cause the temperature in the freezer as a whole to rise which isn't good for the other produce in there. Usually the manufacturer will specify how much can be frozen down over a period such as "12 kg over 24 hours" but as a general rule, never try to freeze down more than 10 per cent of the freezer's capacity in a day. In fact, half that amount is better.

We picked up a cheap electronic thermostat with a probe so that we could check the temperature inside the closed freezer and that it was coping with freezing down fresh foods.

The warmer the food you put into the freezer, the harder it has to work and the longer it will take to cool down. This is why we pre-chill in the refrigerator. Ideally the fridge will bring things down to 5°C (40°F) so the freezer only has to reduce it by 23° whereas from room temperature this could be nearer a 35° reduction – over a third more work.

There are a number of ways to pack into your freezer. The method we favour is to pack into cheap small bags a sufficient amount for one meal. If we have guests, we take out two bags. You can freeze onto trays and then transfer into a larger bag if you prefer, so you can remove as much as you want each time.

The trouble we found with larger bags is that after a while ice forms within and you have a solid block of ice to contend with.

119

However you choose to pack your produce, it is important that it is dry. Hopefully the produce will have drained well but, if it is still damp, empty onto a clean fluffy tea-towel and pat dry before freezing.

Frozen foods must be bagged to exclude air or ice will form around the produce and it will become freezer burnt. Freezer burn is very noticeable on meats. The burned areas will be a different colour and the texture of the meat will be tough. Although not so easily seen, freezer burn will affect vegetables if they are not properly sealed from the air.

If you are packing large irregular shapes, like sweetcorn on the cob or chunks of parsnip for example, then you can insert a straw into the mouth of the bag. Hold the bag tightly around the straw and suck out the air before tying the bag or sealing with a wire twist tie.

Some items are more convenient to pack into plastic tubs and boxes. You can pick up freezer containers very cheaply and if you want to be really frugal we've found old ice cream tubs, margarine tubs and the plastic tubs some takeaway meals come in to be effective. You may find your local Chinese or Indian takeaway restaurant will sell you some of those tubs for very little money if you ask when ordering a meal.

Finally, either label or write on the bag or box what the contents are and the date. In six months' time with a bit of ice on the bag you will not remember if they are runner beans, French beans or peppers in there. You can buy freezer labels on a roll very cheaply. Ordinary sticky labels will fall off as the low temperature stops the adhesive on them from working. For marking you need an indelible felt-tip pen, ordinary felt tip markers will smudge.

Meals

Although we can freeze and store the raw materials for a meal, the freezer enables us to go one better and store entire meals in one go. We've covered some suggestions for soups and side dishes, etc., in the sections on fruit and vegetables but they are only a few ideas. We're sure you'll come up with many more yourself.

Growing your own, storing your own and self-sufficiency are spiritually rewarding, but they do require a lot of work and effort. We've often heard the comment that people don't have time for all that. Well, we have pretty busy lives but we cope and the trick to it is efficiency.

It takes very little longer to make a large pot of soup or a large batch of tomato sauce base than to make a small quantity. Rather than waste damaged potatoes where the slug has had a nibble and we know they won't store well, we turn them into partially cooked French fries or potato croquettes which will save time when we come to cook a meal.

Better still, we might make a batch of potatoes Dauphinoise, one for now and three for the freezer. This doesn't just save time but it makes efficient use of the oven that costs no more to run full than three-quarters empty.

We like the old values of self reliance and the quality of our home-grown and produced foods but that doesn't mean we ignore the benefits of the twenty-first century. If you get home late and tired to find your hungry family is circling like a pack of starving wolves, being able to take a quality meal out of the freezer is a life saver.

Microwave ovens with their magical ability to cook from frozen will defrost and heat a deep frozen dish in just a few minutes. They're also quite efficient in energy usage as the delivered energy to energy input ratio is high.

Incidentally, although we generally use a variety of bags and plastic containers for freezing, there are new breeds of containers becoming available that are worth paying for. Pyrex offer some rectangular glass dishes with a plastic lid. They're ideal for a shepherd's pie or potato Dauphinoise type dish.

Just cook, allow to cool and then place the lid on before freezing. Once removed from the freezer and de-frosted, remove the lid and the containers will go into the microwave or oven to re-heat.

There are also silicone containers coming onto the market that are truly amazing. They can be taken straight from the freezer into a hot oven with no danger of thermal shock breaking them. They'll also go into the microwave. We found it very hard to believe the manufacturer's claims, especially looking at a flimsy tray we thought should melt in the oven, but they're true.

Vegetables – Freezing Quick Information Chart

Globe artichokes
Remove all outer coarse leaves and stalks, and trim tops and stems. Wash well in cold water, add a little lemon juice to the blanching water. Blanch a few at a time, in a large container for 7–10 minutes. Cool, and drain well before freezing.

Asparagus
Grade into thick and thin stems. Wash in cold water and blanch thick stems for about 4 minutes and thin stems for just 2 minutes. Cool and drain, then tie into small bundles, packed tips to stalks, separated by non-stick paper. Generally asparagus doesn't work too well as a frozen vegetable and bottling or making into a soup (see page 138) and freezing the soup works best.

Aubergines (Eggplant)
Peel and cut roughly into 1 inch (2.5 cm) slices. Blanch for 4 minutes, chill and dry on absorbent paper towels. Pack in layers, separated by non-stick paper. You can also fry the slices instead of blanching and then freeze. This doesn't work too well, but is usable in a dish like moussaka and better than wasting a glut.

Broad beans (Fava beans)
Mature beans actually seem to benefit from freezing which softens them if they have become a little tough. Younger, small broad beans freeze well also. Just shell and blanch for 3 minutes before cooling and freezing.

These beans tend to turn the blanching water brown fairly quickly and if you dry on a towel before freezing they may stain your towel. Use an old towel or paper towels if that is a concern.

French (Green) beans
Most varieties freeze very well but some of the waxier types are much better cooked from fresh. Just wash, top and tail and then blanch for 2 minutes before chilling and freezing. Consider salting as an alternative.

Runner beans

These freeze well. Prepare as you normally would and blanch for 3 minutes before cooling and freezing. Consider salting as an alternative.

Beetroot (Beets)

Large beets are normally stored as for root crops but we like the convenience of being able simply to take a small young one ready prepared from the freezer for a salad, so we freeze some small beets for this. Wash well and rub the skin off after blanching. Small beets up to 3 inches (7.5 cm) in diameter need blanching for 10 minutes and larger beets should be boiled until tender for 45 to 50 minutes. A pressure cooker will reduce the time to around 10 to 15 minutes at H pressure and save energy for this.

Freeze the smaller beets whole but slice or dice larger beets or they will take too long to freeze. If you blanch for too short a time, you will find they are rubbery when defrosted.

Broccoli and calabrese

Trim off any woody parts and large leaves. Wash in salted water, and cut into small sprigs. Blanch thin stems for 3 minutes, medium stems for 4 minutes and thick stems for 5 minutes. Cool and drain well. The thick woody stems and leaves will work well in a soup which can be frozen.

Brussels sprouts

Prepare as you would normally. Just remove any outer leaves and wash thoroughly. Blanch for 3 minutes, chill and freeze. When you defrost, they're effectively cooked enough so we just toss in melted butter with salt and black pepper until they're warmed through.

Cabbage

You can freeze cabbage but it tends to be soggy when defrosted, so we cook it like Brussels sprouts. Don't forget that a cabbage will store well for several weeks in somewhere cool, dark but airy. You can also wrap in cling-film and keep well in the fridge for a few weeks.

Wash and shred the leaves, then blanch for just a minute before chilling, draining and freezing.

Carrots

Maincrop large carrots are best stored in sand with the root crops but young, early carrots can be prepared ready to serve, either cut into strips or diced, before blanching for 3 minutes and then chilling and freezing.

With damaged maincrop carrots that will not store well, we make these into carrot mash as covered in Chapter 16, Vegetables.

Cauliflower

Wash and break into small florets, about 2 inches (5 cm) in diameter. Add lemon juice to the blanching water to keep them white; blanch for 3 minutes, cool, drain and pack.

Celeriac

Wash and trim. Boil until almost tender, peel and slice, then freeze when cool.

Courgettes (Zucchini) and Marrows

Choose young ones. Wash and cut into ½–1 inch (1 cm) slices. Either blanch for one minute, or sauté in a little butter. We've found these don't work well but are just about acceptable in a risotto when defrosted.

Fennel

Trim and cut into short lengths. Blanch for 3 minutes, cool, drain and pack.

Garlic

Take peeled cloves of garlic and mince in a food processor with olive or vegetable oil. You need about twice the volume of the cloves in oil. Freeze in ice-cube trays and then store in sealed bags or tubs. When cooking, you can just drop a cube into the dish.

Kohlrabi
Use small roots, 2–3 inches (5–7 cm) in diameter. Cut off tops, peel and dice. Blanch for 1½ minutes, cool, drain and pack.

Leeks
Prepare as normal and then slice fairly thinly (less than 1 inch/2.5 cm). Blanch for 2 minutes or sauté in oil. Cool and freeze. They will be soggy when defrosted but are fine for adding to casseroles or soups.

Mushrooms
Choose small button mushrooms and leave whole, wipe clean but don't peel. Sauté for a minute in butter or oil. Mushrooms larger than 1 inch (2.5 cm) in diameter are suitable only for slicing and using in cooked dishes. Consider drying.

Onions
Can be peeled, finely chopped and packed in small plastic containers for cooking later; packages should be over wrapped, to prevent the smell filtering out.

Small onions may be blanched whole and used later in casseroles. Blanch sliced onions for 2 minutes; small whole onions for 4 minutes.

Usually onions keep well enough in your root cellar that you shouldn't need to freeze them anyway.

Parsnips

Treat just as carrots or cut into chips, blanch for 2 minutes, cool and freeze to make parsnip chips or roast parsnips.

Peas

Process as soon as you can after picking because the sugars are turning into starch when they come off the plant. Shell and put into a pan of cold water. If there are any pea maggots, these will float and can be easily fished out. Blanch for a minute or two at most; shake the basket to ensure heat is evenly distributed. We find it easier just to drop loosely into the pan and fish out with a sieve as they go through the holes in the large blanching basket anyway. Peas freeze really well.

Older peas can be dried or usefully made into "mushy peas", which can also be frozen.

Mange-tout (Snap) peas

Trim the ends. Blanch for 2 minutes, cool, drain and pack.

Sweet Peppers

These actually freeze well for cooking but do go a bit soggy for using as fresh peppers in a salad. Wash well, remove stems and all traces of seeds and membranes before blanching for 3 minutes as halves for stuffed peppers, or in thin slices for stews and casseroles.

Chilli Peppers

Usually we just string and dry chilli peppers but you can freeze them. We had some small round habaneros that for some unknown reason would go mouldy rather than dry. We halved, de-seeded and froze individually on a tray without blanching before packing into bags.

Although freezing usually concentrates spicy flavours, with chilli peppers it seems to make them milder.

Potatoes

Although normally you would store potatoes in sacks, sometimes you have a glut of damaged potatoes that will not keep too well and freezing, if you have room, avoids wasting them.

They are best frozen in a cooked form, as partially cooked French fries (fully cooked ones are not satisfactory), croquettes, mashed or duchesse potatoes. The only method we can recommend as being really good is as French fries. Prepare as usual and part fry in deep oil for 2 minutes, cool and freeze, ready for final frying.

Spinach

True spinach, as compared to beet leaves or perpetual spinach, is another crop that tends to arrive at once. Luckily it shrinks an awful lot when blanched so doesn't take up much room in the freezer. Select young leaves and wash very thoroughly under running water, then drain. Blanch for 2 minutes in small quantities, cool quickly and press out excess moisture. Pack in rigid containers or polythene bags, leaving ½ inch (1 cm) airspace.

Sweetcorn

Corn is one vegetable that is unbeatable when really fresh but it will store fairly well for up to a week in the fridge. If you are not going to use it before that, it is best to freeze. Remove husks and "silks". Blanch small cobs for 3 minutes, medium ones for 4 minutes and large cobs for 5 minutes in plenty of water. Cool and dry.

You can freeze them whole on the cob or cut off the kernels with a sharp knife after blanching and just freeze the kernels in portion bags.

Tomatoes – whole

When the tomato crop comes in we sometimes find we're overwhelmed. Although they can be bottled (canned) well, it's easiest and fastest just to pop them into a bag and freeze them. They're only

useful for cooking after being frozen but there is a benefit in that the skin comes off very easily when they're defrosted, which saves time when preparing.

Tomato – purée

Skin and core tomatoes, then simmer in their own juice for 5 minutes until soft. The easy way to skin tomatoes is to drop them into boiling or very hot water for a minute. After this you will find the skin is very easy to peel away. Pass them through a nylon sieve or, easier still, liquidize and pack in small containers when cool.

Rather than just freeze a purée, you may find it more efficient to freeze tomato sauce base as covered in Chapter 16, Vegetables.

Turnips

Use small, young white summer turnips. Trim and peel, then cut into small dice. Blanch for 2 minutes, cool, drain and freeze. Turnips may be fully cooked and mashed before freezing like carrots.

Freezing Fruit

Fruits are quite easy to prepare for freezing as they usually do not require blanching. Unfortunately, the freezing process will inevitably change the texture of the fruit, those ice crystals rupturing cells again. However, they will be fine to use in pies and puddings or for making jams and preserves. Frozen fruits are also useful for adding to ice cream to make a quick dessert or for sauces and even for babyfoods.

We've covered the correct methods for the common fruits you are likely to have but it's surprising what you can get away with. One morning a friend arrived with two large bags of damson plums for us, just as we were about to go away for a week. We broke all the rules and just put the bags as they were into the freezer. Some months later, we retrieved the damsons and they made some of the best jam we have ever enjoyed.

That admission aside, here's how to freeze fruits correctly for the best results. Fruits will generally keep well for up to a year in the freezer although unsweetened fruits tend to lose quality faster. After this you will begin to notice a deterioration in quality, although they will still be safe to eat. Citrus fruits and fruit juices are best consumed before six months.

The initial preparation is just as you would do before eating or cooking. Sort through and remove any fruits that have damage and wash. Remove any stems and stone where appropriate.

There are three basic methods for freezing fruit: Dry Pack, Sugar Pack and in Syrup.

Dry Pack

Dry pack is where the fruit is just frozen on its own – like our damsons above. The best method to freeze quickly and evenly is to spread the fruit onto a metal sheet or a non-stick silicone sheet if you have one, spaced slightly apart. Once frozen, just put into a freezer bag or a plastic container to store.

Sugar Pack

This method helps keep the texture a little better and provides a readymade dessert. Just add to some ice cream. Of course, there is a lot of sugar involved but sugar is like salt in that moderate amounts are fine; it's excessive amounts in the total diet that are harmful.

Generally prepare the fruit, slicing the fruit and then pack in tubs sprinkling with sugar between layers. The sugar will, over the course of 15 minutes or so, draw the juices out and dissolve into a thick, fruity syrup.

Syrup Pack

Some firm-textured fruits like peaches and apricots are best frozen in sugar syrup. Although some of the vitamins in the fruit can leak out of the fruit into the syrup when thawing, by using the syrup in whatever dish you are cooking, you'll retain the goodness.

Different fruits will ideally need different strengths of syrup to freeze in which are listed below:

Syrup	Approx. % Sugar	Cups of Sugar	Cups of Water
Very Light	10%	½	4
Light	20%	1	4
Medium	30%	1¾	4
Heavy	40%	2¾	4
Very Heavy	50%	4	4

Make the syrup by adding ordinary granulated sugar to hot water in a pan on a gentle heat until all the sugar has dissolved and the water is clear. Allow to cool and then pour into a jug which should be placed in the refrigerator to cool it further to around 5°C when it is ready to use.

Preventing Discoloration

As you've probably noticed when baking a pie, apples will start to brown just minutes after being sliced. They're not the only fruits that discolour when exposed though, pears, apricots and peaches do so as well. Lemon juice is often used to prevent this browning but too much lemon juice can overwhelm the flavour of the fruit.

When freezing, you can prevent this discoloration by using ascorbic acid instead of the lemon juice. Ascorbic acid is just vitamin C and can be bought cheaply as a powder but, if you find it difficult to obtain, use vitamin C tablets and crush into very fine powder with a mortar and pestle. Some tablets will have fillers in that will cause a slight cloudiness in syrups, but it's not really a major problem.

As well as preventing discoloration, vitamin C helps maintain the flavour of the fruits and adds nutritional value, of course. Unlike lemon juice, cooking will reduce the amount of vitamin C, so it is important when adding vitamin C to add it to cooled syrups or cooked fruits that have cooled.

When adding to a syrup, make the syrup up as required and allow to cool, preferably in the refrigerator to 5°C (40°F). Then, just before using, stir the vitamin C in gently to the syrup.

For sugar packs or dry packs, dissolve the vitamin C into a few tablespoons of cold water and sprinkle evenly over the sugar or fruit. Use the amount of vitamin listed under the relevant fruit below.

Fruit – Freezing Quick Information

Apples

Apples will freeze well for later use in pies, crumbles and flans. Peel, core and slice reasonably thickly – we aim for about half an inch (1 cm) thick, cutting out any damaged bits.

As you slice, drop into cold water with added lemon juice to prevent browning. Once you have them all prepared, blanch for just two minutes and cool quickly in iced water with added lemon juice.

To be truthful, we don't worry too much about our apples browning as it won't be noticeable in a pie but we know that many people are concerned. Browning does not mean the apple has gone off.

Pack in a 40 per cent heavy syrup adding ½ teaspoon of ascorbic acid powder to each litre of cooled syrup.

You can sugar pack or dry pack apples.

Usually we freeze some surplus apples in the form of a purée. Just peel, core, slice and stew with a very small amount of water and sugar to taste in a heavy pan. A knob of butter on the bottom helps stop sticking. Mash with a fork and freeze in portions when cool. These are easy to pull out for apple sauce with a pork meal and, with the addition of a little sugar, make a dessert for younger children.

Apricots

Prepare the apricots as you would for the eventual dish, pitting and either halving or slicing. If you are leaving the skin on, blanch for 30 seconds to avoid tough skins when defrosted.

Best packed in a heavy 40 per cent syrup adding ¾ teaspoon of ascorbic acid powder to each litre (2 US pints) of cooled syrup. You can sugar pack but we found the dry pack method did not work well.

Berries and Currants

All the berries, from strawberries to blackberries and blackcurrants, can be frozen. Usually we do this when we're building up enough for a jam making session as the freezing process makes the fruit soggy and unsuitable for eating fresh.

The easiest way is just to prepare the fruit as if for cooking, removing the stalks and hulling strawberries, etc. Then make sure they're dry and spread on a tray and freeze. When frozen pack into bags.

With the larger and juicier berries such as strawberries, loganberries, blackberries, etc., you can sugar pack. Slice the berries in half and the sugar will suck juice from the berries turning into a thick syrup before freezing. If you plan to use for jam, you need to note how much sugar is in the pack. Normally we wouldn't sugar or syrup pack if we were planning on jam making with the fruit.

You can pack berries into a heavy (40 per cent) or very heavy (50 per cent) syrup.

Cherries (Sweet or Eating Types)

Wash and remove stems and stones before freezing. Sweet eating cherries can be frozen in a 40 per cent heavy syrup adding ½ teaspoon of ascorbic acid powder to each litre of cooled syrup.

Cherries (Sour or Jam Making Types)

Wash and remove stems and stones before freezing. These contain less sugar than the sweet types so need to be packed in a very heavy (50 per cent) syrup but you do not need to bother with adding ascorbic acid to the syrup as they are already darker in colour.

Citrus Fruits

You can freeze citrus fruits in a heavy (40 per cent) syrup. Peel and break into the segments if possible, removing any pips at the same time. Cover with syrup and freeze.

It's often more useful to deal with a glut by juicing and then freezing the juice. If you add a little sugar, 30 g per litre of juice (1 oz per 2 pints), it will store better for longer.

The peel of citrus fruits can also be frozen to use as a garnish. Clean off any pith and then cut into julienne strips. Blanch for 1 minute and freeze dry pack or with just a little sugar.

Damsons and Plums

We have found the purée method to be the best for damsons and plums although, as we said above, we've successfully kept damsons for jam for 4 months by just putting them into the freezer in a sealed bag.

You can freeze in a 40 per cent heavy syrup adding ½ teaspoon of ascorbic acid powder to each litre of cooled syrup. Stone and halve the plums before freezing.

Figs

Freeze fully ripe figs, peeled or not as you prefer, whole in a medium (30 per cent) syrup, adding ¾ teaspoon of ascorbic acid powder to each litre of cooled syrup.

Grapes

Grapes can be frozen in a heavy (40 per cent) syrup or sliced in half and sugar packed. However, if you have a volume of grapes, then juicing and freezing may be the better option, unless you fancy wine making.

To make grape juice for storing in the freezer, crush and strain through a muslin sheet or jelly bag to remove the pips and skins, etc. Place into a bain marie and bring up to the simmering point, where a few bubbles appear but not a proper boil, for 10 minutes.

Pour into jugs and allow to cool, then store in the refrigerator overnight. Small crystals will appear and sink to the bottom of the jugs. Pour off the cleared juice and freeze in suitable containers.

Mangoes

Peel and slice straight into a heavy (40 per cent) syrup adding 30 ml of lemon juice to each litre of syrup (1 fl oz per 2 pints).

Melons

All types of melons can be frozen, but they will lose their crispness when defrosted. Cut open and deseed, then cut the flesh into slices or cubes and pack into a heavy (40 per cent) syrup to freeze.

Peaches and Nectarines

The fruit should be skinned and stoned then either sliced or halved as you prefer. You can make the peeling process easier by scalding first but this does encourage discoloration.

They are best packed in a 40 per cent heavy syrup, adding ½ teaspoon of ascorbic acid powder to each litre of cooled syrup (½ teaspoon per quart).

You can sugar pack, adding ascorbic acid to the sugar by dissolving in a little water and sprinkling over.

For purée, heat the prepared peaches in a little water to prevent scorching on the base of the pan for five minutes before passing through a sieve. Add 60 g (2 oz) of sugar and ½ teaspoon of ascorbic acid powder per litre (1¾ Imp pints, 2 US pints) of purée.

Pears

Pears just don't seem to work for freezing except as a purée. Even freezing in syrup resulted in very mushy fruit for us but this may have been due to the pears being slightly over-ripe. We think they're much better bottled or turned into perry (pear cider) but if you want to try, this is the "approved" method.

Peel, core and slice then drop the pears into boiling heavy (40 per cent) syrup for a minute. Remove, drain and allow to cool, then pack into the cooled syrup after adding ¾ teaspoon of ascorbic acid powder to each litre (or quart) of cooled syrup.

Rhubarb

Rhubarb can be frozen but only for later use in cooking. Wash, trim and cut into 1 inch (2.5 cm) lengths. Blanch for one minute, chill and freeze either in a very heavy (50 per cent) syrup or just dry pack if going to be used within three months.

16
Vegetables

•

Globe Artichoke

Globe artichokes can be frozen, stored in oil or bottled in brine.

Jerusalem Artichoke

Jerusalem artichokes will keep well in the ground from November to February. You just need to dig them up when wanted. However, if your ground will be covered in snow or frozen, simply treat as potatoes and store in a sack in your root cellar.

Asparagus

Asparagus is best eaten fresh and in season but being a seasonal crop – and a short season at that – it is either glut or famine. You can freeze asparagus but it does damage the texture somewhat.

Aparagus can be bottled (canned) but here, again, it loses some of that texture that fresh asparagus has.

One way we store our asparagus surplus is to make a concentrated soup and freeze that. Being concentrated, it takes up less room in the freezer. The beauty of this simple recipe is that it uses the tough end of the stem that is usually discarded when preparing asparagus. If using whole spears, reserve the tips which can be blanched and frozen. Keep these with the soup.

Asparagus Soup

1. Take your discarded asparagus stems and gently fry in a little butter for ten minutes or so. Then add either vegetable or chicken stock and simmer. If you make your stock from commercial stock cubes, make it double strength. It's almost the more the better with the quantity of asparagus, within reason.

2. When the asparagus is thoroughly softened, usually after about 20 minutes, liquidize the soup so that no pieces of asparagus are left. Allow to cool and pour into plastic tubs, allowing a little headroom, and freeze.

3. When you are ready to eat your soup, defrost and then add the same quantity of either water or milk, season to taste and serve. If you have some reserved tips these can be added as you warm the soup.

4. If it seems a little thin, add some flour or cornflour (cornstarch) to thicken it a little. We rather like this soup served with a little crumbled cheese mixed in as it is re-heated. If you use a strong cheese, be careful not to overwhelm the delicate flavour of the asparagus.

Broad Beans (Fava Beans)

Once picked, the pod will protect the beans for a week or two, especially if kept cool in a fridge. They are best stored long term by freezing, although they can also be dried or bottled. The blanching process, freezing and defrosting actually improves the texture of older beans that have been left on the plant just a little too long.

French and Runner Beans

These green beans, where the pod is eaten, are generally at their best when eaten young. Picking also encourages the formation of more beans so continual picking will produce a larger crop.

With both French and runner beans there are two main methods of storing – freezing and salting. In fact, these are the only crops that we think worth salting as the end result actually has the edge on freezing as we cover in Chapter 5, Salting.

French beans can be bottled (canned) but we'd urge you to try salting at least some.

Haricot Beans

Haricot beans, including borlotti beans, are the type of bean where the actual bean is eaten rather than the whole pod as with French beans.

Traditionally these are started early to give a long growing season and left in their pods on the plant for as long as possible. Because the British summer is unpredictable at best, at the end of the season the beans are rarely dry enough to store. So the bush plants are uprooted and hung upside down from the roof in a greenhouse or at least under cover, to dry out thoroughly. With climbing varieties, the stem is cut away from the root and then dried on the greenhouse bench.

The other option is to take your partially dried beans and finish them off or dry from scratch in a drying cabinet or oven, etc., as covered in Chapter 13, Drying.

Once dried, the beans can be taken from the pod and stored in airtight jars. Soak overnight in cold water prior to cooking. If you're pushed for time, put the dried beans into a pan of cold water and bring to the boil. Boil vigorously for three minutes and then remove from the heat and cover the pan. Leave in the pan for about an hour and they should be ready to cook as if soaked overnight.

Beetroot (Beets)

Large beets can be stored in sand or peat as covered in Chapter 4, Natural Storage. However, we much prefer to harvest our beets small, just slightly larger than a golf ball. They are sweeter and softer and make a great addition to a salad or as a side vegetable. To store these we either freeze them or pickle them.

Broccoli and Calabrese

Broccoli is very difficult to store. We've found that frozen broccoli is just not up to the job, being soggy at best. Calabrese, which is often mistakenly called broccoli in shops, with its tighter and larger heads will freeze well though and is perfectly acceptable when defrosted.

When preparing for the table or for freezing, quite a lot of the stem is cut off and discarded. However, just as with asparagus, these discarded stems can be used in a great soup.

Calabrese and Stilton Soup

1 onion
500 g (1 lb) broccoli or cauliflower
1 medium courgette (optional)
1 large or couple of smaller carrots (optional)
1 medium potato
30 g (1 oz) butter
2 tbsp olive or vegetable oil
1.7 litres (3 Imp pints, 3½ US pints) water or stock (vegetable)
90 g (3 oz) Stilton cheese (or more to taste, we like loads)

1. Dice the vegetables and add to the pot with the butter and oil and a small amount (about 3 or 4 tablespoons) of water.
2. Heat, stirring to avoid burning, then put the lid onto the pot and cook gently for around 15 minutes to soften the vegetables, stirring occasionally and replacing the lid or shaking the pan to avoid sticking.
3. Add the water, bring to the boil and then simmer gently for around 25–30 minutes.
4. Reserve the liquid and blitz the vegetables in a food processor or put through a Mouli grater.
5. Return to the water and crumble in the Stilton cheese and season to taste.

This recipe also works well with cauliflower, including discoloured cauliflower, and you can make it using half the water and freeze the "concentrated soup" adding water or milk to bulk it back up before serving.

It will work with a weak chicken stock as well, but this gives us a meal that is vegetarian friendly if we have veggie visitors.

Stilton is quite an expensive cheese and can be hard to obtain outside of Britain but any strong-flavoured, hard cheese will do. If you do use Stilton, then be aware you can use the hard rind that is discarded when eating it. We often use much more cheese than the recipe actually calls for, which makes it a very hearty soup.

Brussels Sprouts

Brussels sprouts will stand for some time on the plant or you can harvest by cutting off the entire stem which will keep the sprouts themselves fine for a couple of weeks if kept cool and dark.

For long-term storage, freezing is the best option. Don't forget when you come to cook them that there are few more awful vegetables to eat than sprouts that have been boiling away for hours.

We take our sprouts and allow them to defrost to room temperature and then just quickly fry in butter or olive oil until warmed through before seasoning with salt and freshly ground black pepper. The sprouts have already been cooked enough by the blanching process.

If the idea of frying fills you with cholesterol horror, then just steam until the sprouts are heated through.

Cabbage

We use the word cabbage to cover quite a variety of plants, from the loose leafed to the tight ball head type. The ball heads store best. Remove the loose outer leaves and check carefully for hiding slugs and snails. If you suspect you've missed a few of the pests, rub a little salt on the outside of the cabbage. Store on slatted shelves or suspended in net bags in your root cellar (see Chapter 3, Where to Store) where they will be happy for a couple of months.

Most cabbages are too big to eat in one sitting. If you use half and tightly wrap the rest in cling-film it will keep in good condition for at least a couple of weeks in the fridge.

You can freeze cabbage. It isn't ideal, but if you have a damaged plant or a loose leafed cabbage, freezing is an option.

Red cabbage does, of course, make a wonderful pickle (see Chapter 10, Pickles) and cabbage is the base of sauerkraut (see Chapter 6, Lacto-Fermentation).

Carrots

There are two basic types of carrot: the maincrop that is bred for size and storing; and the early that is designed to come to maturity early and be eaten young, sweet and small.

When we grow our carrots, we allow the seedlings to develop a little before thinning out. These immature thinnings are very tasty – you'd pay a fortune for them in a restaurant. With these and early carrots, the best way to store them is by freezing. Just prepare them for serving (we simply scrub under running water rather than peel), and blanch for a minute or two, depending on how large the carrots are. Cool and freeze into portion sized bags.

For the main crop carrots, sort into those that are perfect and those that are damaged. Particularly towards the end of the season, the slugs have a nasty habit of nibbling the top of the root. The longer anything is in the ground, the more chance some pest will have had a go. Unfortunately, it's an inevitable outcome of home growing, unless you use the chemical armoury available to the farmer, which we think defeats the object of growing for yourself.

Damaged carrots should be prepared for serving, cutting away and discarding the damaged parts and then frozen. With the larger sizes and tougher texture of maincrop carrots, blanch for 3 to 5 minutes before cooling and packing.

Another method of freezing damaged maincrop carrots that we favour is to make carrot mash. Clean and discard damaged parts and then dice the carrots quite small. Cook in just enough water to cover or steam until soft. Add some butter and mash using a potato masher and season with a little salt and pepper. Pack enough for a portion into plastic tubs and freeze.

The advantage of this is that there is no wasted space and it saves time when you are preparing a meal as all you need to do is re-heat and serve. There are variations on this dish where the carrots are mixed half and half with parsnip or swede (rutabaga).

Cauliflower

Once cut, a cauliflower will last for a week or so if kept in a cool, dark place but can be kept in good condition for three or four weeks if tightly wrapped in cling-film and kept in the refrigerator.

Do watch out for slugs, caterpillars and sometimes earwigs hiding deep in the florets. Even in the refrigerator they'll still be munching away, albeit slowly.

The best way to store long term is by freezing. Cut into small florets, about 2 inches (5 cm) in diameter. Wash thoroughly before blanching for 3 minutes. Adding some lemon juice to the blanching water will help to keep the florets white.

Cauliflower is a basic ingredient of piccalilli and goes well in a number of chutneys. It can also be bottled (canned).

Courgettes (Zucchini)

Courgettes are notorious for producing gluts, especially with new growers who happily start off a dozen plants and then find that they have a crop that would feed a small army later in the year.

Unfortunately, they're not a crop that's easy to store. You can freeze them but they don't cook well afterwards. You can use them in pickles and chutneys though or in a soup and freeze that. Next year, grow fewer!

Cucumber

Cucumbers will keep quite well in the salad container of the refrigerator and you can extend the life by tightly wrapping cut ends in cling-film to reduce water loss. Cucumber cannot be frozen due to its very high water content. We did come across a method of storing cucumber by salting but we can't recommend it – the end result was poorly textured and still very salty after washing. Cucumber is perhaps one of those crops best enjoyed in season, although you can, of course, use up a glut of cucumbers in pickles or chutneys.

Garlic

Garlic stores really well with little effort and, with a little luck, this year's crop will keep until next year's crop is ready. After harvesting, dry as you would onions, but don't forget you can use fresh garlic or "wet garlic" almost as a vegetable. The garlic flavour is concentrated by the drying process so wet garlic isn't that strong a flavour.

After drying for a week or so, trim any long roots and hang in a cool, dry place, taking a bulb as you need. Traditionally, the stems would be platted producing the decorative strings often seen in the greengrocers. However, the easier method, and in some ways more effective, is just to tie the stems together a few inches above the bulb and hang them using the string. Just cut the stem when you need a bulb.

The other method you can use is to put them into a net – the leg cut off an old pair of tights will do. Don't put too many into one bag though as you need to allow air to circulate or they will be susceptible to rot.

Garlic cloves can also be stored in oil (see Chapter 14, Storing in Oil) or frozen (see Chapter 15, Freezing) but properly dried bulbs, hung in a cool, dark place with some airflow will keep until the next crop arrives.

Leeks

Leeks are very much a winter vegetable and will stand quite happily through the harshest of British weathers. However, in really cold weather you can find they are impossible to dig up from frozen ground. You may also want to dig over the space they've occupied as you prepare your vegetable plot for the spring.

You can heel in your leeks which will keep them in good condition for a couple of months. Just dig up the leeks and then dig a shallow trench a few inches deep, with the soil heaped to one side of the trench. Place the leeks side by side in the trench so they are leaning at about a 45 degree angle and fill with loose soil or compost.

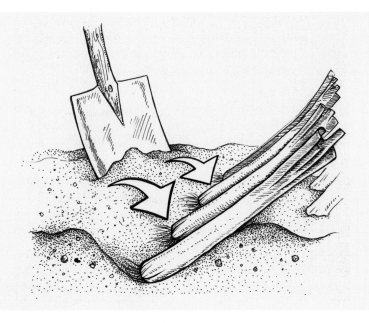

In effect they are being kept alive as if standing still in their planting spot but taking up much less room and they are far easier to pull if the ground is frozen. In really cold climates with deep snow covering, "heel in" to a bucket of damp soil or compost kept under cover in a garage or cellar.

You can freeze leeks but blanching in water really does tend to make them soggy and watery when defrosted. The best way is to prepare the leeks by removing the tops and roots, then cut into 1 inch (2.5 cm) slices and rinse well to remove any grit. Sauté in hot oil or butter for 4 minutes then drain, cool and freeze. You will have lost quite a bit of texture but they're perfect for adding into a casserole or into a soup.

Lettuce

You can't store lettuce as such but you can prolong its life after harvest. Often you don't use a whole lettuce at one meal and by the next day the remainder is looking decidedly limp and unappealing.

Instead of cutting the lettuce, pull it up with the roots attached. Use the leaves you want immediately and then put the roots into a vase of water, keep the lettuce in a cool place out of direct sunlight and it will keep well for at least a week.

In recent years the supermarkets have been supplying salad leaves in bags which have quite a long shelf life. The way they produce these is not something you would want to duplicate at home, I hope.

First of all, the salad is washed to remove any soil and pests that may be lurking – often in a bath of what is, in effect, dilute bleach. They are then packed in an inert gas, 99 per cent nitrogen so that there is no oxygen to fuel spoiling bacteria before being shipped. And some people actually think the flavour is acceptable!

Onions

To ensure that onions store well, you need to dry them properly to start with. After harvesting spread the onions onto a wire frame or netting, spaced as far apart as you can, to allow air to flow around them. In rainy weather you need to provide some sort of cover as they won't dry if they're being soaked in water.

When the weather is really against you, dry them indoors on a netting frame or slatted shelves. If the air is going to be still, then a fan will help no end. Many electric fan heaters have a fan only setting. You mustn't try to heat them at all though; slow drying at room temperature is the aim.

One bad weather year, we attempted to dry them off in a greenhouse. This was fine until we had one hot, sunny day and the temperature shot up, filling the greenhouse with the smell of cooking onions. The crop was pretty much ruined.

Be aware that larger onions will take longer to dry, often three times as long, as smaller onions. The very large onions you see in shows may have taken months to dry properly.

If you have any rot starting on an onion, particularly white fluffy mould on the base, the onion will not store for long and can pass this onto other onions nearby. Use any affected onions first or consider drying them. (See Chapter 13, Drying.)

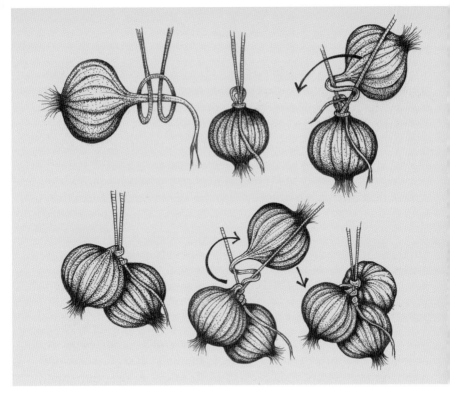

Before stringing your onions, trim any long roots back to about an inch from the bulb with scissors. This is a good opportunity to double check for rot and any softness which may indicate it hasn't dried properly.

The best way to store onions is using the traditional string. It's complicated to explain, but once you have done it a couple of times you will find it simple and quick to do.

Take a length of string and double it. Next make a loop at the base and feed the first onion into that. Hang the string from a nail to continue; it's a lot easier.

The next onion leaves are threaded through the double rope and then those from the one after are threaded in the opposite direction, alternating until your string is full. Through, around and down is what we repeat to keep the technique in mind. The illustration should help to explain.

The other method, less elegant but still effective, is just to tie a bunch of half a dozen or so together from the stem as suggested for garlic.

We've seen onions stored in nets and in the legs of tights but find the stringing method is actually easier. Also the onions keep better with the greater airflow that stringing allows. Do hang them in a cool, dry and dark place. Dry is particularly important to prevent rotting and mould growth. Just bring a bunch at a time into the kitchen when you are ready to use them.

There is, of course, one other way of preserving onions. Where would we be without pickled onions? (See Chapter 10, Pickles.)

Parsnip

Parsnips are a very hardy vegetable and you can safely leave them in the ground through the harshest of British winters. In fact, when they have had a few hard frosts the flavour improves as, like the potato, starches turn into sugars and the parsnip becomes sweeter.

However, digging up your parsnips when the ground is frozen solid can be impossible and you can't leave them in the ground when spring arrives. In the spring, parsnips will use the energy in the root to throw up a seed head and reproduce themselves. This ruins them as a crop.

Parsnips will store well in sand or peat in the shed – see Chapter 4, Natural Storage.

If you only have a few parsnips to keep or some damaged ones, you can freeze them. Cut into strips or chunks and blanch for 2 minutes before cooling and freezing. You can then use them in soups and stews or for roasting or frying. For frying, treat them as you would potato chips and fry from frozen.

Peas

For young sweet peas, you really can't beat freezing. We found that they slipped through the holes in our blanching basket so now we just tip them straight into the blanching water and then fish them out with a sieve. They only need blanching for 1 to 2 minutes at most. Of all the vegetables, young peas are the ones that really need to be blanched fast and cooled quickly for the best result. Don't attempt too many in one blanch. Freeze quickly in small quantities.

Recipe

1. Soak the dried peas overnight; they should triple in volume when thoroughly soaked.
2. Place in a covered pan with some chopped mint and simmer slowly, stirring occasionally and topping up the water if necessary, until they are really tender.
3. When cooked, add a finely chopped onion, fried until tender in butter, and a little extra butter if the peas seem a little dry. Salt and pepper to taste. Allow to cool and then freeze in portion sizes in rigid containers.
4. If you prefer, and we do, run through a food processor before freezing. To serve: defrost and warm in a pan adding a little cream just prior to serving.

Incidentally, if you make this from a packet of dried peas, don't add the tablet of bicarbonate of soda that comes in the pack as it reduces the nutritional content. It's true they break up better with bicarbonate of soda added but it's better to use the food processor if you like them sloppy.

Peas can be bottled and, of course, you can dry young peas instead of freezing but it seems a shame when they're so nice from frozen. With older, more starchy peas you can dry them or you can make your own mushy peas – just like the chip shop's but better – and freeze them.

The above recipe uses dried peas but with fresh you just omit the overnight soak.

Chilli Peppers

Chilli peppers are very easy to dry, you don't need any special equipment and they will keep for well over a year. Take a darning needle and make a hole through the stem and then thread onto thin wire. You can pick up a roll of thin wire in most garden suppliers very cheaply.

Hang your chilli peppers up somewhere warm and dry and that's it, job done. To retain their colour, keep them out of direct sunlight. Be aware when cooking them that drying seems to concentrate the hotness of the peppers.

When dry, you can leave them strung but if you need the space, grind in a mortar and pestle or use a food processor if you prefer. Store as chilli pepper in airtight jars.

Chilli peppers can be stored in the freezer. For long-term storage they need to be blanched for about a minute, being generally much smaller than sweet peppers. If you are just storing for a few weeks, then you can omit the blanching process. Freezing does seem to reduce the hotness of peppers, although with habaneros and those really super-hot peppers some people like to grow, it's difficult to tell since they're so hot to start with.

Do be careful when processing chilli peppers. If you don't like wearing gloves to undertake fiddly tasks like removing seeds, ensure you wash your hands very thoroughly afterwards. Touching your eye with even small traces of chilli pepper on your hand is excruciatingly painful.

Fresh or dried chilli peppers will also store well in oil, see Storing in Oil, Chapter 14.

Sweet Peppers

Sweet peppers will keep for a few weeks to a month in a fridge. For longer storage freezing is fine, although they will be more use in cooked dishes rather than salads as they lose their crispness when frozen.

They can also be stored in oil (see Chapter 14, Storing in Oil) and bottled.

Potatoes

It is perfectly possible to store your home-grown potatoes from harvest until the next crop comes in. Your first **early** potatoes (which people often call **new potatoes**) often grow quite large if left in the ground and store well. We've enjoyed "Swift", a very early variety as the name suggests, right through to the new year.

With the wet summers that we seem to be having more frequently nowadays, growing early potatoes is becoming more productive than main late crops. The main crops may yield more per square yard but the early types miss the blight that damp weather engenders and so you actually get a usable crop.

Potatoes are best harvested early, on a dry, sunny day if possible. This means you can leave them on the surface for a few hours to harden the skin. If it's one of those years where getting a couple of decent days together seems impossible, you can spread them in a cool greenhouse or even on the garage floor for a day or two.

The next job is to sort them out into two piles: those for long-term storage and those for using first. The best potatoes for storing are perfect, with no holes or wounds from the fork when harvesting. Just brush off the dirt as you check them over. There's no need to wash them until you are ready to eat them with one exception. If blight has struck your crop and the spores have got to the tubers, they will rot in store. You can significantly reduce the incidence of blight in your stored potatoes by washing them with just a drop of detergent in the water.

Potatoes with small holes, where a slug has got in, or with other damage will not store as well, so put these into a "use first" bag.

Potatoes store best in a hessian sack (burlap bag). These can be bought quite cheaply from garden and seed potato suppliers. The reason is that the potatoes in store will release moisture and the sacking material allows them to breathe whilst excluding light.

Light will, over time, cause your potatoes to turn green. The green potato contains alkaloid chemicals, solanine and chaconine which are poisonous, so you shouldn't eat green potatoes.

If you find that some of your potatoes are more than a third green at harvest – perhaps they've worked themselves onto the surface when growing – discard them. Less than a third green are worth keeping as they will lose the green if kept in absolute darkness. You should cut away any green in skin or flesh you find when preparing for a meal.

If you don't have a hessian sack available, you can try paper sacks. A friendly chip shop may well give you some for the asking. They're not ideal for our purpose but will do in a pinch. We've also used old pillowcases as potato sacks.

When using last year's hessian sacks, especially if you've had some blight or rot in the sack, it's a good idea to give them a wash. They tend to shed so we wouldn't recommend using the washing machine. A bath full of hot soapy water with just a splash of bleach will sterilize them adequately for another year.

Never, ever, store potatoes in plastic bags and especially not in transparent or white ones. Not only will light get through but moisture will not escape and your potatoes will rot quite quickly.

When the potatoes are placed into the sack, it's a good idea to drop a few slug pellets in. It's surprising how many times you miss a little hole in a "perfect" potato and a slug is inside the hole. Not only will he eat that potato but he's bound to creep out to damage a few others. Slug pellets contain an attracter which entices them out to eat them and stops further damage. The potatoes will be perfectly safe and there is no danger to pets or wildlife as the pellets are in the sack.

Empty out the sack after a month and check that none of the potatoes is rotting in store. In a bad blight year there is bound to be one that has got through and blight spreads very easily from one to the other in store. If you are unsure of a potato, smell it. Blight has a

Duchesse Potatoes

1. Take 1.5 kg (3 lb) peeled potatoes, after discarding any bad parts, and boil in salted water until tender. Drain and mash well or pass through a potato ricer.
2. Mix in 150 g (6 oz) of butter and season with salt, pepper and nutmeg if you like.
3. Next mix in 2 beaten eggs. If the mixture is a little dry add some cream or milk to achieve a good consistency.
4. While still warm, feed through a piping bag with a fluted nozzle to make elegant portion sized cakes on a greased baking tray.
5. Freeze and store in containers.
6. To serve, place the cakes on a greased baking tray and brush with beaten egg before placing into a hot oven, 220°C (425°F/Gas Mark 7) until browned and cooked through – usually 10 to 15 minutes.

very distinctive unpleasant smell that you cannot confuse with anything else.

One year when we were checking over our potatoes before bagging them, we noticed that flies were attracted to potatoes that appeared perfect to the eye. These turned out to have soft spots starting to rot. It was a bad year for blight. We assume the flies knew which ones were starting to rot from the smell.

The sacks themselves should be stored in a cool, dark place. The ideal temperature for storing potatoes is between 5° and 10° Celsius (40–50°F).

Too warm will reduce storage life but too cold can be worse. Below 5°C the starch begins to turn to sugars and the potatoes will develop an unpleasant strange sweetish taste. Bringing them into the warm (around 15°C/60°F) for a week or two will usually cure this.

If the temperature has fallen around freezing or below, the potatoes will not only taste strange but become mushy and probably start to rot when the temperature rises.

If you have damaged potatoes that you know you will not be able to use before they go off, then you can freeze them. You can't freeze them just as potatoes but you can make duchesse potatoes, croquet potatoes or chips and freeze those. Ordinary mashed potato can be frozen, just make as normal and shape into patties. Freeze the patties and store in an airtight bag until required. Be aware the texture isn't quite the same and they often seem watery, so use as a topping for dishes like shepherd's pie and bake in an oven until browned on the top.

Frozen Chips (French Fries)

To store as chips, peel and cut into chips discarding any bad bits, then deep fry for 2 or 3 minutes. Remove from the oil and place onto a tray to cool then freeze on the tray. The oil should stop any sticking. Once frozen, bag up into portion sized bags, removing as much air as you can. You don't need to defrost them before cooking, just deep fry until brown.

Salsify and Scorzonera

With both these superb but sadly under-grown vegetables being root crops you would expect them to store like parsnips but our experience is they deteriorate very quickly. They are best stored by freezing. Prepare and then blanch for 2 minutes in water with lemon juice added to keep the colour. Cool and freeze.

Shallots

We've always considered shallots to be an under-rated vegetable, if only for the fact that they store so well and fill that gap between the old onions passing their best and the new onions coming in. Our experience is that they can store in excellent condition for eighteen months, so going off in store just isn't a problem.

Like onions they need drying before storing but their smaller size means this is an easy process even in a bad weather year. We suspect it is their smaller size that is responsible for them storing so well.

They are too fiddly really for stringing but are easily tied into bunches or you can store in net bags as for onions and garlic. Like onions they can be pickled, which is a good use for a glut of shallots. If you do have plenty of shallots, don't forget that you can re-plant them instead of buying new sets for planting.

Spinach

Spinach is a great vegetable to freeze as it reduces a lot when cooked. Just prepare by removing any browned leaves, etc., and cut up a little to make it easier to handle. Wash well in a colander and then drop into a large saucepan on a low to medium heat without drying off the spinach. You will not need to add any water as there will be enough water on the leaves for cooking.

Keep stirring and it will reduce tremendously in volume. Remove from the pan and squeeze any excess water out before freezing in containers or bags.

Squash and Pumpkin

When you harvest, cut the stem a couple of inches (5 cm) from the fruit; not tight to the fruit as this is where rot inevitably seems to start.

The key to storing butternut squashes and pumpkins is curing them after harvest. In an ideal world, a week or two in the late autumn sunshine will harden off the skin, sealing and protecting the flesh within. A properly cured squash will have a skin so hard that it will resist scoring from your thumbnail.

We lay ours out on a slatted garden table in a sunny spot. This allows good airflow around the fruits and helps dry them off if we have a shower or two. Every couple of days, rotate the fruits bringing the shaded side to the sun.

Once cured, they move into our cool, dark root cellar onto the slatted shelves. Different varieties will keep for different times and pumpkins don't tend to keep as long as the squashes, so we use our pumpkins first and then move onto the squash after they've gone. The squash will last right the way through to late spring.

Swede (Rutabaga)

Swedes will store in sand or peat just like the carrots and beetroots. However, they have a tendency to dry out more, so if you can keep them in a separate box, keep the packing material a little damper than you would normally.

They don't last as long as carrots and beets in store – usually just a few months. So keep a close eye on them and use them up before they go over.

Sweetcorn

Sweetcorn is the one crop that really is best eaten fresh but it doesn't lend itself to a long cropping season. While you can sow many vegetables in succession, this is not possible with sweetcorn. It needs a long growing season and crops started late may well be killed by autumn frosts before the cobs are ready.

Unless you have a huge vegetable plot, you shouldn't grow different varieties of sweetcorn in the same year as they can cross pollinate. Especially with F1 hybrid varieties, this can result in poor development, with many kernels failing to develop. So it isn't possible to grow different types which mature early and late.

All of this means that the whole crop comes in over a very short period, just a couple of weeks. You can try drying sweetcorn by just leaving the cobs on the plant to dry naturally but that's pretty uncertain in the British climate. Freezing really is the best option by far, allowing you to enjoy something very nearly as good as fresh sweetcorn throughout the year.

Sweetcorn can be bottled and it's always nice to make a few jars of sweetcorn relish for the store cupboard.

Tomatoes

The tomato is probably the most popular vegetable to grow at home in the UK, despite it being vulnerable to pests, diseases and the whims of the weather. Even greenhouse grown tomatoes are subject to weather as the tomato relies on heat and sunshine to ripen on the plant. Because of this uncertainty we tend to start more plants than we need so when we have a good year, to say we have a glut is an understatement.

Apart from a summer glut, at the end of the season most of us find that we're left with green tomatoes on the vine but without the time for them to ripen before the first frosts arrive.

Of course, you can use them up in a green tomato chutney but they also provide a way for you to extend your fresh tomato season right the way through to Christmas. Choose the tomatoes that are fully developed and about ready to change colour and ripen rather than the very immature ones which can go into your chutney.

When you pick the tomatoes, green or ripe, break off the stalk at the knuckle rather than pulling the tomato away from the calyx (the green leaves attached to the fruit) as they will keep for longer this way.

The ideal temperature for storing green tomatoes is 12–13°C (54–56°F). They also need to be kept dark, so we use a drawer in our

Spicy Tomato Cooking Sauce

We were sent this recipe, which freezes well, and found it a real time-saver. It's very versatile. For example, you can cook chicken pieces in it or use it as the base of a curry. If you are not sure how spicy you would like it, instead of the quantities given below, add 4 teaspoons each of the cumin and coriander and 4 pinches of chilli powder, allow the spices to infuse for 5 minutes, then taste. You can also add roasted peppers – or green beans sliced small.

Olive or vegetable oil as required

500 g (1 lb) onions, sliced

4 big cloves of crushed garlic

2 kg (4 lb) tomatoes (roughly quartered or chopped depending on size)

6 teaspoons ground cumin

6 teaspoons ground coriander

6 large pinches of chilli powder

4 tablespoons tomato purée

1. Put the oil, onions, and garlic into a large pan. Cook them until just soft.
2. Add the tomatoes and cook them until they start looking mushy. Add the cumin, coriander and chilli powder, sprinkling it over and stirring well, then lastly add the tomato purée to thicken it.
3. Keep it gently simmering for about half an hour in total until it is a lovely thick creamy texture.

Lasagne Sauce Base

This simple recipe really concentrates the flavours and is useful for more than just a lasagne. It makes a good base for a Bolognese sauce or a pizza. There are no fixed quantities, which means that each batch differs from the one before thereby giving freshness to the eventual dish. Adjust the thickness of the sauce by adding water if required.

Tomatoes – to cover a baking tray
Onions
Herbs (basil, bay, etc., to your taste)
Red wine
Salt and pepper

1. Cut up the tomatoes, chop the onions and place both in a large, deep oven tray. Add the herbs, pour on the red wine, season and cover with foil.

2. Bake for about 1 hour in a medium oven. There is no rule: it's ready when it is all well softened.

3. Liquidize and pour into containers allowing some headroom, cool and freeze.

unheated spare room. Place some tissue paper or slightly crumpled old newspaper in the drawer to hold the tomatoes firmly and place them stalk upwards so that they don't touch.

They will continue to ripen, albeit slowly, in there so check weekly. If you need to speed the ripening process, take out some tomatoes and place in a bowl with a ripe banana in the warmth of the house. The ethylene gas will speed the ripening process along and they'll be red in a few days.

Normally for health reasons we would promote eating raw fruits and, where appropriate, raw vegetables as cooking does reduce vitamin content but with tomatoes they may actually be better for you cooked. That's not to say you shouldn't enjoy vine-fresh sun-warm tomatoes on their own or as a side dish.

Tomato Soup

Tomato soup is so warming on a cold winter's day. There's nothing better than drinking summer's warmth when there's frost on the ground. You can make the soup as in the recipe or use less stock and freeze after step 5, continuing the process when defrosted adding more stock or water.

1 onion
2 stalks celery
1 carrot
800 g (2 lb) tomatoes
1 litre (1¾ Imp pints, 2 US pints) vegetable stock or water
Salt and pepper
1 sprig parsley
1 bay leaf
6 peppercorns
25 g (1 oz) butter
25 g (1 oz) flour
150 ml (5 fl oz) milk

1. Peel and slice the onion finely. Chop the celery and carrot into small pieces.
2. Fry the onion, carrot and celery lightly in a little butter or oil in a large pan.
3. Slice the tomatoes and add them to the other vegetables, along with the stock or water, salt and pepper and the parsley. Tie the bay leaf and peppercorns in a piece of muslin and add to the pan.
4. Bring to the boil and simmer gently until the vegetables are tender.
5. Remove the muslin bag and either push the mixture through a sieve or put through a blender.
6. Melt the butter in a pan, add the flour, blend well and cook for a minute or two without colouring.
7. Gradually add the tomato purée, stirring all the time.
8. Bring to the boil and cook for at least 3 minutes, stirring constantly.
9. Add the milk and re-heat without boiling. Serve hot.

The reason is that tomatoes contain a chemical called lycopene. Lycopene is a powerful antioxidant and studies have indicated it may well reduce the risk of getting cancer, especially prostate cancer. Raw red tomatoes are a good source of lycopene but cooking breaks down cell walls, releasing and concentrating the chemical. Tomato sauce may well contain twice to four times the lycopene found in the raw fruit.

Tomatoes can be dried and then stored in oil, bottled or frozen as well as converted into chutneys, relishes and ketchup. The best ones to use for bottling are the plum varieties, notably Roma and San Marzano. They're not particularly good for eating as raw tomatoes but they are fantastic when cooked.

Freezing is a convenient way to store tomatoes, either whole or as a purée. However, if you are going to purée them you might as well go a step further and prepare a sauce base that will save you time when you come to make a meal.

We've included a couple of our favourite tomato sauce recipes.

Turnip

Turnips can be frozen or stored in sand or peat like carrots. It's best to store younger turnips in the freezer unless you are dealing with a large quantity.

17
Fruits

●

Apples

Until relatively recently, at least in tree years, apple trees of one fruiting variety were most often grafted onto vigorous rootstocks from other trees or crab-apples. This was because many great fruits were growing from naturally weak trees and grafting enabled strong growing trees whatever the natural inclination of the fruiting part.

Nowadays we're fortunate in that the home grower can buy the flavour of apple they want but grafted onto various dwarfing rootstocks, enabling small but still strong trees to be grown.

But if you have an old apple tree in your garden – in fact the same goes for most fruit trees – then you are going to have a huge glut each year. Just to complicate the problem of coping with that glut is that some apples will keep better than others. There are literally hundreds if not thousands of different varieties, so listing them all and their keeping qualities is well beyond the scope of this book.

However, as a general rule, the later in the season a variety matures, the better the apple is likely to store. Knowing when your apples are mature is a matter of judgement as well. Different weather conditions through the season will affect maturity.

When the apples look ready, full sized and ripe, then pick one to check. It should be easy to pick by holding the apple, lifting upwards and twisting. Don't just tug the apple off as you'll damage it – damaged or bruised fruit will not store for long.

If you harvest too early, the apples will be tart and sour but leave them on the tree for too long they'll become woolly and mushy. Not all the apples mature at exactly the same time on the tree – usually from start of maturity to the last one being ready takes a week or two.

Don't worry though. After a while it becomes second nature to pick the ripe apples by eye and leave those needing a few days longer. Do be gentle with them. Place them in your basket; don't throw them down from the tree. Remember, bruised apples will rot in store.

Those that are bruised or damaged need not be wasted. They can be frozen, bottled or turned into juice and cider.

The grand Victorian estates with their private kitchen gardens could afford special apple houses to store their harvest. Rows of shelves with the different varieties carefully labelled in dark climate controlled rooms. So the "big house" could always have juicy, perfect apples in the fruit bowl on the table. Nowadays the commercial suppliers have air-conditioned warehouses with controlled atmospheres instead of an apple house.

The ideal storage condition for apples is a temperature just above freezing, ½°–1°C (33°–35°F), and a humidity between 80 and 90 per cent. Increase the temperature by just 5°C (or 10°F) and you may reduce the storage life by a third or more. Too dry an atmosphere will cause dehydration and wrinkling of the fruit.

As you can see, it's pretty challenging to achieve the perfect conditions at home so in practice we just store them in the coolest dark place we have along with the vegetables.

Place on shelves, stalk upwards, with a little space between the apples so they don't touch. Don't store in closed drawers or the like as this will allow the build up of ethylene gas and will increase the rate of deterioration.

Depending on the variety and the conditions in your store you can realistically expect to keep your apples in good condition for anything between 40 days and three months. Once you see them starting to go over, consider the other storage methods such as bottling, freezing and drying and juice or cider.

Pears

Pears are completely different from apples in that they do not ripen on the tree. In nature they fall to the ground where they ripen and are eaten by the wildlife to spread their seeds. So judging the correct point to harvest is something of an art.

Once the fruit have reached the correct size, you should notice a lightening of the skin colour. Another indicator is that the small whiteish spots on the skin, known as lenticels, will darken to a brown colour.

Fruit left on the tree for too long may start to taste gritty. This is due to stone cells starting to develop in the fruit. The flesh may discolour as well.

The fruit will still be firm when you harvest, but handle with care. Even more than apples, pears bruise easily although this may not always be apparent on the skin, only being discovered when you come to eat them.

The ideal storage conditions are similar to apples: at a temperature just over freezing with high humidity. Generally pears do not store for as long as apples but it really depends on the variety.

Unlike apples, which are ready to eat when harvested, you need to ripen pears yourself. It's very easy. Just bring them into the warmth of the house for 3 to 10 days. You actually want a temperature between 15° and 21°C (60–70°F) to ripen pears properly. Too high a temperature may soften the flesh too much and cause browning.

If you are in a rush, pears can be ripened more quickly by putting them into a plastic bag with a ripe banana. The build-up of ethylene gas speeds the ripening process.

Other options for storing pears are: bottling, freezing, drying and perry (pear cider).

Citrus Fruits

Citrus fruits will keep for a week or even two at room temperature, a month or more in the refrigerator. To handle a glut, juicing the fruit and freezing the fruit juice is one option, bottling another or you could turn some of your surplus into marmalade.

Berries
Blackberries, Loganberries, Raspberries, etc.

The problem with berries is that, once picked, their storage life is very short. They contain a lot of sugars and the shape of the berry is perfect to encourage moulds. In as little as 24 hours at room temperature a bowl of blackberries can be developing mould. Even storing in a refrigerator won't extend life for long, perhaps an extra day or two. So eat or process berries as soon as they are harvested. Berries can be frozen, bottled or turned into jam. A lot of people enjoy the flavour of berries but find the pips somewhat annoying, so consider making a jelly instead of a jam where the pips are strained out.

Don't forget the wonderful combination of blackberry and apple in pies and crumbles.

Cranberries, Blueberries, Lingonberries, etc.

Although called berries, these are more like currants and will store for up to a week in a refrigerator. However, the faster they are processed, the better. Cranberries and lingonberries will make excellent jelly or sauce to use with meats and poultry. With blueberries, bottle or freeze for use in pies, etc., later.

Cherries

The cherry falls into two families: the sweet cherry for eating fresh; and the sour cherry, like Morello, for eating cooked or making into jam. However, don't waste a glut of sweet cherries. They can be bottled or frozen for use in pies, etc., as well.

Apricots, Peaches and Nectarines

These are superb bottling fruits. You can make jams or conserves with them but the results tend to be too sweet and the texture is somewhat mushy. Bottled in syrup they are a great ready-made dessert, served with a little ice-cream. They also dry well – dried apricots make a healthy snack that tastes sinful.

Strawberries

Strawberries are best, in our opinion, enjoyed fresh but they do make superb jams and conserves. Because they tend to arrive in flushes, we freeze those that we can't eat immediately and, when we have enough, turn them into jam. You can bottle strawberries, but we think they are better in a jam.

Currants
Blackcurrants, Redcurrants, White currants

All the currants make outstanding jams and jellies. They can be frozen for later use but since they tend to come in one go rather than over a period, we just make them into preserves.

Blackcurrants are a good bottling fruit and you can make an easy "cheats" blackcurrant liqueur. Just fill a bottle with washed, de-stalked blackcurrants and every so often lightly crush a few with the handle of a wooden spoon. Once filled to near the neck, fill up with brandy and cork or cap the bottle. Pop into the back of the cupboard for six months or so.

Not only a great liqueur, the brandy-soaked berries with a sorbet make a sophisticated adults-only dessert.

Rhubarb

You really shouldn't have a glut of rhubarb. By growing different varieties and forcing for the earliest, sweetest crop, your fresh rhubarb can cover quite a long season. Rhubarb will freeze satisfactorily for incorporating into pies and crumbles but for the best texture, for eating as a dessert, bottle it.

Plums and Damsons

Both these have a fairly short life when harvested but can be frozen for later use in cooking or for making into jam. Different varieties will affect the flavour of jams more than you might expect. We have two friends who donate damsons in return for jam and one is OK but the other is brilliant. That's worth bearing in mind if you are buying trees.

Plums bottle well for later use in desserts and both freeze well.

Figs

Figs should be stored in the refrigerator but even there they have a short shelf life of just a couple of days. They can be frozen or bottled.

Pineapple

Pineapple doesn't keep for long. You may get a week from home-grown cut pineapple before you notice the quality deteriorating. Opinions are mixed on refrigerating. Certainly they should be kept in cool conditions. The best method of long-term storing, if you're lucky enough to have a glut, is bottling in syrup.

Grapes

Those Victorian master gardeners had a problem in that the proprietors of the big house would make unreasonable demands for dessert grapes months out of season. To accommodate them, they would leave the bunches of grapes on the vine for as long as possible in the heated vinery and then cut off whole bunches with a good length of stalk. These were placed in a bottle of water into which charcoal was mixed to keep it clean and fresh. There were even special bottles, shaped rather like the bottles the nurses brought round to

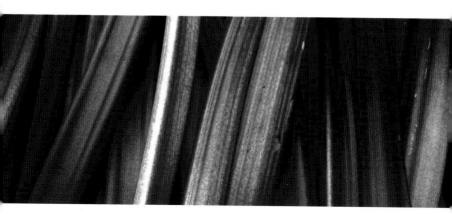

bed-bound men in hospital, which allowed the bunch of grapes to hang down whilst the stalk was in the water although wine bottles were frequently used for the task.

The grape room was cool and dark but not humid as mould was the great enemy. By using late fruiting varieties grown in heat and careful attention to the store, they almost managed to have fresh grapes on the table year round. Fresh stored grapes in April or even May were not unusual.

The most efficient way to store grapes nowadays is either as grape juice or, of course, wine.

Melons

Melons will keep for two weeks in the refrigerator but they are difficult to store long term. They can be frozen in syrup, but the result certainly loses texture. They are low acid and should not be bottled. Theoretically they could safely be bottled using the pressure method but the result is an inedible mush.

Mangoes

Mangoes will ripen quite quickly in the presence of ethylene gas so, to ripen them, put a pair into a plastic bag or a mango with a ripe banana. Once ripe they will keep in the refrigerator for two weeks. They can be frozen but mangoes do make excellent Indian chutney and pickle.

18
Herbs

●

Herbs are often considered as secondary in the garden. Mainly they're easy to grow and don't require a lot of attention so they almost get ignored. However, in the kitchen they're vital. Just look through your recipe book and see how often they say add a sprig of thyme or a bouquet garni.

Providing a supply of herbs for the kitchen all year round is less challenging than you might at first think. Some herbs are, of course, available all year round anyway. Keeping a bay tree in a pot by the kitchen door is not only decorative but useful as well.

With some herbs it's perfectly possible to keep a fresh supply available by growing in pots on the kitchen window sill. The following list can all be grown indoors in pots to provide a fresh supply even in winter:

- Basil
- Chervil
- Chives
- Lemon Grass
- Marjoram
- Mint
- Parsley
- Thyme

The main and traditional method of storing summer herbs for winter use is drying but with some soft-leaved herbs, that are best used fresh, freezing is a way to get that fresh herb flavour into a dish at any time of year.

Always pick your herbs for both drying and freezing at their best. Waiting until they are past their best just means you're spending effort on an inferior product. Pick your herbs just before they come into flower as after flowering the leaves start to toughen up.

Even the type of day and time of day you pick can make a difference. Ideally you want to pick on a sunny day, preferably early in the morning when the volatile flavour oils are at their strongest as the sun hasn't evaporated them off.

Freezing

The reference books suggest blanching herbs tied into a bunch for a few seconds and then cutting or chopping into small pieces. Place these into ice-cube trays, top up with water and then freeze.

Having tried this, there was a little loss of flavour which we think was down to the blanching process so now we omit the blanching. With chives we just wash and chop before packing into the ice-cube tray and then top up with cold water and freeze.

With herbs like basil, where they are pretty much dissolved in the final dish, we found this method quick and easy, especially when coping with a large amount.

Wash and strip the leaves from stalks where appropriate. Put the leaves into a blender and add about a quarter by volume of water and whiz into a paste before transferring into an ice-cube tray to freeze. To use, just drop a cube or two into the dish as you cook.

Drying

Drying herbs is really quite easy and doesn't require a drying cabinet or machine. Drying does tend to concentrate the flavour and for some recipes dried herbs are actually preferable to fresh. They're certainly convenient. We keep ours in the cupboard by the stove where they are always handy to add to the pot whilst cooking.

Pick your herbs as described above and then remove any dead or withered leaves. Tie them into small bunches with thin string or cotton. Blanch very quickly by dropping into boiling water for no more than five seconds.

Blanching does seem to help speed the drying process, but we've successfully dried herbs without blanching so feel free to omit this step if you're pressed for time. However, it is a good idea to give your herbs a rinse under running water to clean off any dust, etc., before drying if you're not blanching. Shake off the excess water and then pat dry with a towel or kitchen paper.

There are number of factors that will affect the time it takes to dry your herbs thoroughly. Temperature is obviously important. They will dry faster in the warmth. However, you don't want to over-heat them. Gentle warmth such as that found in an airing cupboard or over a heating boiler (furnace in the US) or cooker is sufficient. Of course, you can use a commercial dryer or homemade drying cabinet as long as the heat is gentle.

Airflow is also very important for drying herbs. You don't need a fan but you do need somewhere where the air is circulating.

Finally, watch for humidity, especially when drying in a kitchen. Your herbs will never dry properly in a damp atmosphere. We hang ours in the kitchen near the stove, which has an extractor for steam when we're cooking.

You don't want your herbs covered in house dust so lightly wrap in some muslin or other loose-weaved light fabric like cheesecloth to protect them whilst drying. It can take anything from a few hours to a couple of weeks to dry thoroughly, depending on the herb and the conditions. You will know they are properly dry when the main stems of the herbs crack, rather than bend, and the leaves are brittle.

If you are in a hurry or do not have anywhere to air dry them, you can dry herbs in your microwave. This is a simple and easy process but you do need to pay careful attention to what you are doing. Lay two sheets of absorbent kitchen roll paper and then put a layer of herbs down, then another layer of paper towel. Use the microwave on high for 1 minute and then in bursts of 30 seconds, moving the herbs around and checking dryness frequently.

Allow time between each burst of microwaves and do not over-heat them. The whole process should take no longer than 5 minutes with spaces between each burst of heating.

Herbs can also be dried in a conventional oven so long as it can be run at a cool enough temperature. Sometimes you may find you need to run the oven with the door slightly open to keep the temperature from rising too high. If so, never leave it unattended especially if there are curious children or pets around. The correct temperature ranges between 45°C/110°F/Gas Mark 0 and 55°C/130°F/Gas Mark 0.

Ideally place on wire mesh racks in the centre of the oven and turn a few times to ensure even drying.

Once dry you can hang them in decorative but useful bunches in the kitchen to pick from as required. It is more practical though to strip leaves from the stems and then crush the herbs with a rolling pin, discarding any stalks. If you want to reduce them to a fine powder, sieve them.

They will store well (so long as they are thoroughly dry) in small airtight containers, well-filled to preserve the fragrance. If stored in glass bottles, protect them from the light to conserve the colour or look for brown glass bottles. If the herbs are not very well dried when stored this way, they will develop mould. Otherwise they will store well for a year or even a couple of years in jars.

Common Kitchen Herbs

Basil
Easy to grow in pots for continuous fresh supply otherwise best frozen as described above.

Bay
Fresh leaves can be picked all year round but dried bay with the concentrated flavour is actually superior in some dishes.

Borage
Best fresh or cut up and frozen in ice-cubes. Not suitable for drying.

Chervil
Pot grow for continuous fresh supply or freeze or dry.

Chives
Pot grow for continuous fresh supply or freeze.

Coriander
Leaf coriander can be frozen or dried.

Dill
Pot grow for continuous fresh supply or freeze or dry.

Lemon Grass
Pot grow for continuous fresh supply or freeze.

Marjoram and Oregano

Some varieties can be pot grown indoors but they dry well.

Mint

Can be pot grown indoors in winter for fresh, frozen or dried. Mint can also be stored as mint sauce base which will keep for six months. Take 285 ml (½ pint) of malt vinegar and dissolve 175 g (6 oz) of sugar in it over heat and boil for 1 minute. Then add 100 g (4 oz) of washed and chopped mint leaves and stir well. Allow to cool and pot into clean jars and seal. When you want some mint sauce, just thin some of your base with vinegar to the desired consistency and serve.

Parsley

Perfect for successional pot growing, can be frozen or dried.

Rosemary

Usually available year round fresh from the bush. You can dry rosemary but best not crumbled into jars. Leave in sprigs that can be removed from the dish before serving.

Sage

Will do well in a pot for continuous supply. Can be frozen but best dried.

Tarragon

Best dried rather than frozen.

Thyme

Suitable for window sill pot growing. Can be frozen but more usually dried.

19
Eggs

●

Although this book is primarily about storing vegetables, fruit and herbs, increasingly people are keeping some poultry in the back garden and enjoying those delicious fresh eggs. So we thought it worth including some help on handling and storing those eggs.

Because hens and ducks lay seasonally, producing more in the summer than the winter, in the summer you can find yourself with a glut and short in the winter. Three laying hens can provide 21 eggs a week in season yet just six or so in the depths of winter.

The first rule is to keep your eggs in date order. We just use old egg boxes from the shop in a row and fill from the left to the right. As a box on the left is used, the empty moves to the right for the latest eggs. Whatever system you use, it's important to have some system to keep track of their age or one day you'll find yourself with rotten eggs in the pan.

The best place to keep eggs is in the fridge at around 5°C (40°F). Eggs kept in a basket on the counter in the kitchen may look attractive, but their storage life will be far shorter and condition will deteriorate quickly. At 21°C (70°F) significant deterioration will be noticeable after just a week.

When you come to use your eggs, remove from the fridge a few hours in advance to allow them to come up to room temperature.

This is particularly important when making mayonnaise or meringues.

If the eggs are clean, you'll find that they will keep well for 10 weeks or more in the fridge. In fact, they may keep for several months this way as the egg is an incredibly well packaged product. The quality of the egg does start to deteriorate though after 10 weeks and you'll notice they don't work so well when making mayonnaise and the white becomes much runnier and less defined when frying, etc.

Incidentally, if you enjoy a boiled egg for breakfast, it is better to use eggs that are a couple of weeks old. With very fresh eggs, removing the shell from the egg is difficult. The reason is that when the egg is laid, the white and yolk are covered in a thin membrane which lies next to another thin membrane just under the shell. When peeling, these membranes stick together and removing the shell without damaging the white becomes almost impossible.

As the egg ages, evaporation occurs through the porous shell and splits the two membranes apart, making it easy to peel. This actually gives us an easy way to estimate the age of an egg. Very useful when someone helpfully tidies up the fridge and messes up the egg date storage system!

If you are unsure of an egg's age, you can find out with a bowl of water. As the egg ages, an air pocket develops at one end which increases its buoyancy. Gently place your egg in a bowl of cool water. If it lies flat, then it is very fresh. If it rises at one end, it is less fresh. If it stands on end, then it is really time it was used. If the egg floats off the bottom, it's too old to eat.

The system isn't foolproof. You may have an egg that is fairly fresh but the hen has been keeping it warm by sitting on it and it's gone off or started to develop if fertile.

Dirty eggs, where the hen has defecated on them, may not store so well and could even harbour bacteria that have passed through the shell so these should be used within 30 days and cooked well. Never eat dirty eggs raw in mayonnaise, etc., in case a bit of shell falls in whilst cracking it.

Although commercial producers may well wash eggs, this does tend to reduce the shelf life. The egg shell is slightly porous and washing may actually introduce bacteria into the egg. If you don't want to store dirty eggs in your refrigerator, which is understandable, then wash them quickly in hot water containing some detergent, rinse in hot water and then dry off. Don't do too many at a time and change the water frequently. Don't rinse your eggs in cold water as this will cool the interior of the egg and may cause a drop in pressure, sucking bacteria from the shell into the egg.

You can, of course, trade or give away your surplus eggs. But when the winter comes and you discover that you are short of eggs, some in store is a real boon. There are some traditional methods that can be used to store eggs which we will cover for the sake of completeness, but the most convenient has to be freezing.

Freezing Eggs

Just placing your eggs in the freezer will cause the interior to expand as it freezes, breaking through the shell and creating a real mess. The way to freeze eggs is to break the eggs, separating the white from the yolk and then to pour into ice-cube trays. Usually two ice cubes of white and one of yolk will equal one fresh egg.

Splitting the yolks from the white is really useful if used for cooking as you can just use whites for meringues, etc., or just some yolk to thicken a sauce, etc. If you are using your eggs in savoury dishes, you can add a little salt before you freeze which helps prevent a skin developing when you defrost the cubes.

Frozen eggs can be used in most dishes where you would use fresh but the texture of omelettes can be a little leathery and they can be difficult to get a good texture when whipping for soufflés, etc.

Painting Eggs

One old method of storing whole eggs was to paint the shell with gum Arabic mixed half and half with water. The gum blocks the pores in the shell, preventing evaporation and the eggs will store for quite a long time but it is messy and time-consuming to do. If you miss a bit, then the egg will not store any better than an unprotected egg.

Salting Eggs

One of the delicacies of Chinese and Asian foods are salted duck eggs. The eggs are covered in a paste of salt and charcoal and kept for months. They can also be dry packed in cooking salt or a brine solution. While it does work in preserving the egg, the result is really quite an acquired salty taste.

Waterglass

Before refrigeration was commonplace, whole eggs would be stored in crock pots in a waterglass solution for up to six months. Waterglass is sodium silicate and the solution is made by mixing 1 part sodium silicate with 9 parts water.

Finding waterglass is quite tricky nowadays, although some pharmacies will order it in for you. Do not confuse it with isinglass, a product used in home winemaking.

If you want to try this method and don't have a suitable crockery pot, then a food grade plastic bin will suffice.

Keep the pot in a cool place and the eggs should be fine for six months but do be aware that a hairline crack in the shell will be enough to allow the egg to go off. Crack the eggs into a cup before using just in case. This used to be common practice but we've become complacent nowadays as the commercial egg quality and age is far better controlled.

Pickling

Pickled eggs are still very popular in Britain and a jar of pickled eggs can be found in most traditional chip shops and pubs. They make a great tangy snack, especially when washed down with a pint of best bitter. We've included the method in the chapter on pickling.

20
Conversion Charts

●

Y ou would think that converting between different measurement systems would be a simple matter of mathematics and, in one sense it is, but cooking and preserving aren't an exact science. A chemist may well measure out 454 ml but the cook will have a measuring jug and fill to the 450 ml mark, or the 16 fl oz mark.

Recipe writers often take this into account and may offer a recipe in two systems, say imperial and metric measures, rounding the measures to the nearest sensible amount. Because of this it is very important not to mix the two systems when using one recipe: ½ lb to 1 pint may have been "duplicated" as 250 g per 500 ml so using 250 g in the pint would be wrong as ½ lb is actually 225 g.

When converting a recipe from one system to another, do your calculations before you start cooking and pay special attention to the ratios, as in the ½ lb to the pint example above. We've learned from experience that sitting down with pen, paper and a calculator can save you from disaster like putting in 10 times the amount of salt the recipe actually needs.

Oven Temperatures

Modern electric forced air ovens deliver heat more efficiently than conventional electric ovens so, if you have one, you may be able to reduce the temperature. For bottling (canning) using the oven method, it is a good idea to check with an oven thermometer what the actual temperature is of the oven.

Gas Mk	°C	°F
Mk ½	120/130°	250°
Mk 1	140°	275°
Mk 2	150°	300°
Mk 3	170°	325°
Mk 4	180°	350°
Mk 5	190°	375°
Mk 6	200°	400°
Mk 7	220°	425°
Mk 8	230°	450°
Mk 9	240°	475°

Spoon Measures

Technically there is a slight difference in US and imperial teaspoons and tablespoons but practically this can be ignored.

1 teaspoon = 5 ml	1 tablespoon = 15 ml

Liquid Measures (Volume)

1 imperial fluid ounce is equal to 0.96 US fluid ounces – so near that for practical purposes you can ignore the difference for small quantities. However, a US pint is significantly smaller than an imperial pint as the US pint has 16 fluid ounces against the imperial 20 fluid ounces.

Imperial	Millilitres
1 fl oz	28 ml (count as 30 ml)
2 fl oz	56 ml (count as 60 ml)
3 fl oz	85 ml
4 fl oz (¼ Imp pint)	114 ml
8 fl oz	235 ml
10 fl oz (½ Imp pint)	285 ml
18 fl oz	510 ml (say ½ litre)
20 fl oz (1 Imp pint)	570 ml

US	Millilitres
1 fl oz	30 ml
1 pint (2 liquid cups)	473 ml
1 quart	946 ml (usually just taken to 1 litre)

Dry Weight Conversion

Imp. Weights	Metric
½ oz	14 g
1 oz	28 g
1½ oz	42 g
2 oz	56 g
3 oz	84 g
4 oz	112 g
5 oz	140 g
6 oz	170 g
7 oz	200 g
8 oz	225 g
9 oz	253 g
10 oz	280 g
12 oz	335 g
14 oz	392 g
1 lb (16 oz)	450 g
2 lb	900 g

Cups

Many American recipes use cups for dry ingredients which are an accurate measure of volume (8 US fl oz) but not of weight. For example, a cup of flour is usually quoted as 5 oz or 140 g but sifted flour with more airspace might be as little as 100 g. For preserving, where the measurements need to be reasonably accurate, we'd suggest sticking with a pair of weighing scales.